Jane Webb Smith

**An exhibition at the
Valentine Museum, Richmond, Virginia
April 5 - October 9, 1990**

Published by the Valentine Museum
April, 1990

Distributed by the University of North Carolina Press,
Chapel Hill, North Carolina

Support for this exhibition and
catalog provided by a major grant
from the National Endowment for the Humanities,
a federal agency.

Catalog Design: Lisa Cumbey, Design Manifesto, Richmond, Virginia
Cover Illustration: J. Alan Cumbey, Design Manifesto, Richmond, Virginia
Photography: Robert Ziegler, Richmond, Virginia
Editor: Nancy Growald Brooks, Arlington, Virginia
Printing: Satterwhite Printing Company, Inc., Richmond, Virginia
Typesetting: Molly Bell, Richmond, Virginia
Exhibition Design: Chester Design Associates, Inc., Washington, D.C.

CONTENTS

As part of a long-range planning process in 1984-1985, the Valentine identified its principal intellectual thrust through 1992 as a reinterpretation of the city's history — using the scholarship of the past 25 years in urban and social history as a perspective. Hitherto, much of the history written about Richmond treated the city in isolation and tended to take an idiosyncratic view of its past. A central task in the museum's reinterpretation of the city's history was, therefore, to locate Richmond in the mainstream of American history, identifying those developments that were typical of most American cities and those that were particular to Richmond.

The museum and its scholarly consultants broke this very large research task into a series of 16 manageable research and exhibition projects to be developed from 1985 to 1990 and mounted as temporary exhibitions from 1986 to 1991. These projects are regarded as "works in progress" toward the reinterpretation of Richmond's history, including the reinstallation of the Richmond history galleries scheduled in 1992. While complete in themselves, these exhibitions and related catalogs and essays allow the museum to test its arguments and designs, solicit additional information and objects, and receive criticism from the public and the scholarly community.

At the same time that individual members of the museum's staff pursued these special research projects, the entire staff embarked on a seminar-based review of the literature of American history. As research findings were reported to the seminar, larger themes in American history began to be linked to the projects.

Because tobacco has a central place both in Richmond's history and its mythology, consideration of the industry was essential when the museum laid out its agenda of projects focusing on important gaps in the history of post-Civil War Richmond. *Smoke Signals: Cigarettes, Advertising and the American Way of Life* became the obvious vehicle to consider four clusters of scholarship. Although curator Jane Webb Smith's two years of research in over 30 collections, including the massive holdings at Duke University, the National Museum of American History, the New-York Historical Society, the New York Public Library and the corporate archives of American Tobacco, R.J. Reynolds, and Philip Morris contributed to the scholarship on the tobacco industry, her essay and exhibition are also important as a thoughtful synthesis of the work of cultural, economic, and business historians. The curator and the museum are deeply indebted to those scholars whose work we used.

Three approaches to scholarship place the cigarette industry in the center of developments that revolutionized American life between the Civil War and the Great Depression. Alfred Chandler's *The Visible Hand: The Managerial Revolution in American Business* was especially helpful in placing the tobacco and cigarette operations in Richmond in the context of the creation of the modern corporation. If viewed from the 20 square blocks of Tobacco Row, Richmond seems to be at the very heart of the cigarette industry. Chandler's work, however, allows us to see Richmond as only one link in a chain that depended as much on the creation of a mass market and wholesale and retail distribution systems as on the manufacturing process itself. Even the nature of that manufacturing was prototypical of processing industries, which gave birth to American corporate giants.

The creation of the necessary mass market for mass-produced goods, the development of a national advertising industry, as well as the related question of industrial design, are the themes of a second cluster of scholarship. These developments were mostly outside of Richmond but the city's cigarette trade was dependent on them. Especially important to this section were the Winterthur conference *Accumulation and Display: The Development of American Consumerism, 1880-1920*; Roland Marchand's *Advertising the American Dream*; Michael Schudson's *Advertising, The Uneasy Persuasion*; Jeffrey Meikle's *Twentieth Century Limited*; Richard Guy Wilson's, Dianne H. Pilgrim's, and Dickran Tashjian's *The Machine Age in America, 1918-1941*; and the Henry Ford Museum's *Streamlining America*.

The transformation of American values from those of a "producer society" to those of a "consumer society" is the focus of a third body of scholarly and critical literature. The work of Robert Wiebe, John F. Kasson, Jackson Lears, and Daniel Horowitz laid the foundation for *Smoke Signals*' historical argument in part four of the essay and exhibition. The critics of this transformation range from antebellum clerics to conservative contemporary politicians and even mammoth corporations themselves.

Consideration of values is nowhere more important than in studies of Richmond. It can be argued that since 1945 no part of the country has experienced the rapid advance of the consumer society as has the urban crescent of Virginia from Fairfax through Richmond to Norfolk. This region was long seen as a slow southern backwater. Richmond especially was viewed as frozen in Civil War time, its Lost Cause nostalgia creating a paralysis of will. Recently, however, former governor Gerald L. Baliles inadvertently riled local citizens with his view that Virginia was no longer a southern but a middle-Atlantic state.

A lack of self-confidence and ensuing conservatism permeated the city after the war — forces with more potency than the financial devastation wrought by the struggle. While antebellum Richmond had been the hub of the nation's third-largest rail system and had quickly upgraded its technology as new developments came on the market, postwar industrialists were unwilling to meet the challenge of the emerging new corporation described by Chandler. A lack of capital, a desire to control former slaves, and a social conservatism reinforced by the Lost Cause myth made the city hesitate, Hamlet-like, before its choices. One example of this loss of self-confidence is the massive Tredegar Iron Works. The center of the Confederacy's weapons production, it never made the move from iron to steel.

Nowhere is this failure of nerve more evident than in the cigarette industry. Richmond manufacturers underwrote the invention of the machine that made mass production of "smokes" possible. But they let it go to James Duke because they did not believe it possible to sell so many cigarettes. As a result, Richmond workers received millions and millions in wages, but the billions and billions in profits were largely shifted outside of the city and state.

One goal of the Valentine's series of 16 "work in progress" exhibitions is to solicit advice and criticism. Early in the run of this exhibition a public symposium with several consultants and critics will be held and videotaped. That tape will then be available to visitors to the exhibition. Previous experience with this format of "public editing" of the museum's work has shown that we can expect valuable contributions from experts and the public alike.

We have a special debt to Cary Carson, Scott A. Ellsworth, Stacy Ann Flaherty, Daniel Horowitz, T.J. Jackson Lears, Michael S. Schudson, Susan Smulyan, and Richard Guy Wilson, who served as referees of the manuscript and exhibition script. Marie Tyler-McGraw, historian of the Richmond History Project, has been deeply involved in this project as she is in all of our work. The readers provided much useful criticism and suggestions to improve the exhibition and this essay. The museum is gratified that they expressed such general approval and enthusiasm for the results of Jane Smith's work.

Some members of the public have raised the question "Why isn't this exhibition directly focused on the issue of cigarettes and health?" The answer is simple: cigarettes and health is a subject about which the Surgeon General, the Tobacco Institute, the tobacco industries, and a host of others have fully informed the American public. *Smoke Signals* notes this debate where it touches the subject of this exhibition. The creation of a consumer society and the revolution in American values are much less widely known subjects. The museum believes that it has an important public responsibility to provide a scholarly historical context for the discussion of these issues.

The Valentine hopes that visitors will leave *Smoke Signals* as interested in American values as they are about American health.

Frank Jewell
Director
Valentine Museum

ACKNOWLEDGEMENTS

In curating this exhibition, I feel that I have been a coordinator on two levels: that of ideas in synthesizing the scholarship of others on four large and complex topics and in the field of advertising art, where I have been the beneficiary of others' longtime enthusiasm for cigarette and tobacco advertising ephemera, artifacts and audio/visual material — of which I never knew there was so much! With the help of many, many people, I was able to create a project that met with the approval of the National Endowment for the Humanities. I thank the Endowment for that support.

A very patient group of consultants read this essay during the busiest time of the academic year. Some, in fact, have read it twice! I would like to thank Cary Carson of Colonial Williamsburg Foundation; Stacy Flaherty and Scott Ellsworth of the National Museum of American History, Smithsonian Institution; Daniel Horowitz of Smith College; T.J. Jackson Lears of Rutgers University; Michael Schudson of University of California in La Jolla; Susan Smulyan of Brown University; and Richard Guy Wilson of University of Virginia. Of this group a special thanks goes to Stacy Flaherty, who, since this process began over two years ago, has been cheerfully willing to talk to me on the telephone — sometimes daily — while keeping up with two babies and a heavy travel schedule.

Frank Jewell and the staff of the Valentine must be recognized for their unwavering commitment to the long-term goals of the museum. *Smoke Signals* is but one of the 16 "works in progress" that will contribute to the scholarship of the future Richmond history galleries, but each project is approached with the same goals of excellence. They are a bright, talented group of people, and I'm proud to be part of the team.

In the early stages of research for this project, I chose three major tobacco companies with which to work. All three have been very cooperative, and I wish to thank the individuals who donated time and loaned artifacts to make *Smoke Signals* possible: The American Tobacco Company: Kathy Coolidge, John Hager, Randy Hart, Jan Hodges, Charles H. Mullen, and Gerald B. Newmark; for Philip Morris, U.S.A. in Richmond: Terry Lynn, Robert J. Moore, Patricia A. Wells; Philip Morris Companies, Inc. in New York City: Karen Brosius, Stephanie French, and Kay Galleotti; and at R.J. Reynolds Tobacco Company: Barry K. Miller and Seth Moskowitz.

Special thanks go to the lenders, both individual and institutional, who are listed on page 6. There are, however, many workers behind the scenes in these organizations with whom I have spoken over the years, and who have made sure that the object did in fact reach its destination at the Valentine. I would like to thank Peter Daniels and Nanci K. Edwards, Agricultural Division, and Fath Davis Ruffin and Cheryl Washer, Archives Center, National Museum of American History, Smithsonian Institution; Clifford Sisson, Department of Special Collections, University of Virginia; Sarah P. Nevue, The American Advertising Museum; Janice McNeill and Louise Brownell, Chicago Historical Society; David Wright, Museum of Tobacco Art and History; Samuel W. Price, National Tobacco Textile Museum; Ellen G. Gartrell and Linda McCurdy, Manuscript Department, William R. Perkins Library, Duke University; Innis H. Shoemaker and Nancy Quaile, Prints Department, Philadelphia Museum of Art; Judy Edwards and Lynn Poirier-Wilson, The Strong Museum; and Bill Chamberlain, Virginia State Library and Archives.

Other individuals who have shared their time, enthusiasm, and knowledge with me are Dale Coats, Duke Homestead; David G. Altman, Ph.D., Health Promotion Resource Center, Stanford University; Catherine Heinz, Pioneers Broadcast Library; Linda Cohn, Liggett & Myers Tobacco Company, Inc.; Marvin Safir; and Linwood Hines III, Conclave of Richmond Pipe Smokers. Special thanks must go to Joseph C. Robert, author of primary sources on Richmond's tobacco history, and Ben Rapaport, "tobacconist" *par excellence*.

In conclusion, I would like to thank my friends and "consultants" Barbara and Cary Carson, for their support and for the comforting feeling that I always have a "port in the storm."

Jane Webb Smith
January 8, 1990

The period from 1880 to World War II ushered in changes that continue to shape the way we live. Industrial mass production called for radical innovations in the distribution and marketing of great quantities of goods. Expansion beyond a regional market was essential and was facilitated by a managerial revolution. A new "visible hand," or middle manager, coordinated the flow of raw materials and finished goods from fields and mines through factories to consumers from a headquarters usually located in a large urban market.

Mass advertising was critical to the creation of a national market that transformed America from a culture of producers to one of consumers. The foundations of modern business, mass production, mass distribution, and mass marketing orchestrated by a network of corporate offices had been established by the turn of the 20th century and grew in complexity throughout the century.

America was transformed from a culture urging self-restraint to one built on immediate gratification through ownership of goods and pursuit of leisure time. This revolution in American values created choices for the new consumers that were foreign to their American heritage. New social thought offered advice to the bourgeoisie, the factory worker, and the new woman shopper. These advisers helped them adjust to the new psychological and material demands of the culture of abundance, which promoted self-definition through the ownership of specific goods. Many of these demands were created by advertising agencies.

Smoke Signals: Cigarettes, Advertising, and the American Way of Life considers this critical period in American economic and industrial growth and uses Richmond's cigarette industry as a vehicle to explore the managerial and second industrial revolutions, the development of American advertising, and the transformation of American values.

Tobacco was and remains important to Richmond. Tobacco was the bulwark of Virginia's economy for over two centuries and Richmond was the hub of the market before the Civil War. By the 1880s, however, conservatism associated with the "Lost Cause" made Richmond businessmen suspicious of new technology that they associated with Northern urban materialism. Continuous-processing machinery, first used in agricultural processing industries such as tobacco, was rejected by local cigarette manufacturers unable to believe that a market existed for mass-produced cigarettes. Richmond's insular vision during this critical period of growth for the rest of the country dictated its economic future for much of the next century. Tobacco remained a central employer, but tobacco leadership and profits left the city forever.

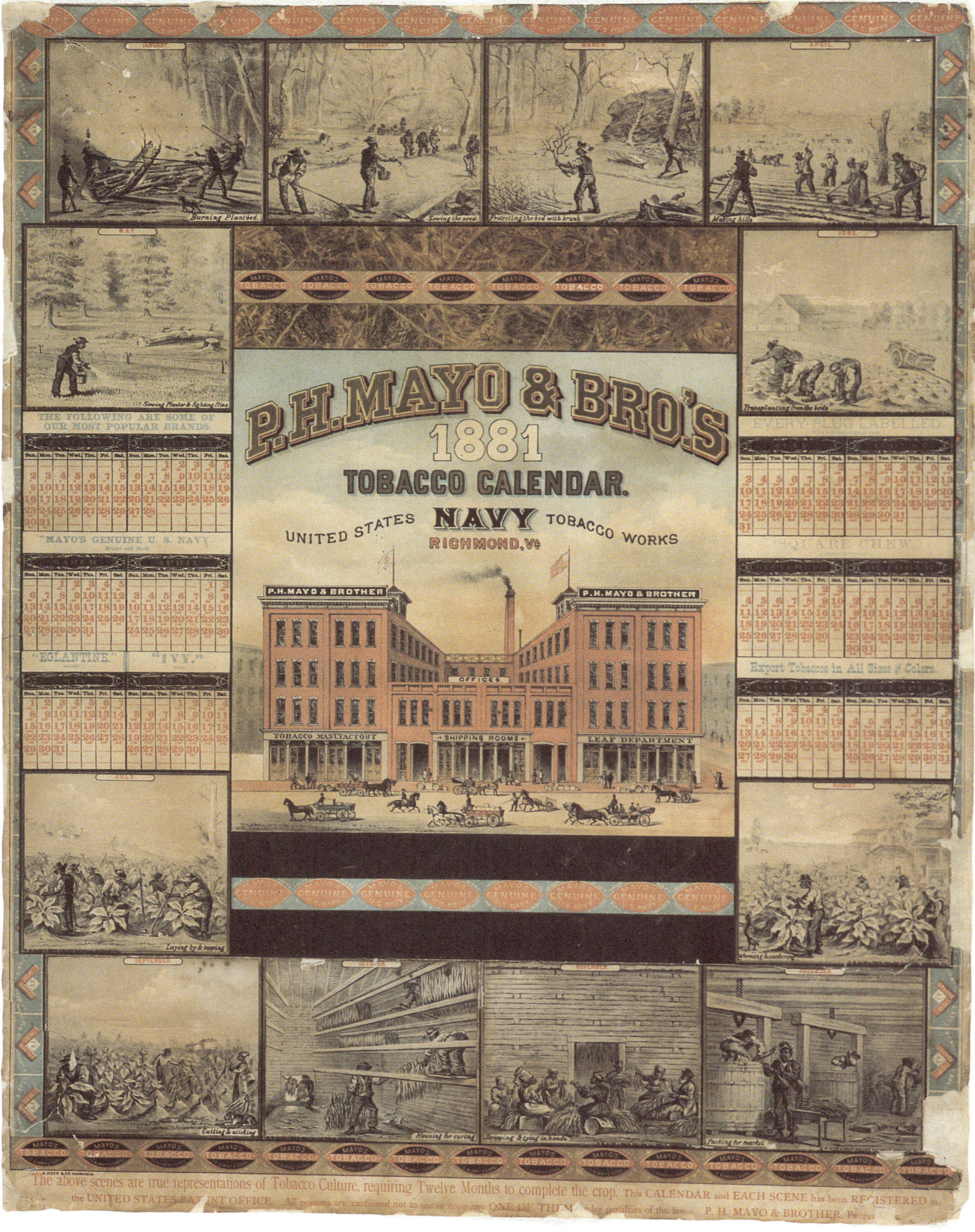
P.H. MAYO & BRO'S
1881
TOBACCO CALENDAR.
UNITED STATES NAVY TOBACCO WORKS
RICHMOND, VA.
P.H. MAYO & BROTHER
P.H. MAYO & BROTHER
OFFICES
TOBACCO MANUFACTORY
SHIPPING ROOMS
LEAF DEPARTMENT
JANUARY.
FEBRUARY.
MARCH.
APRIL.
MAY.
JUNE.
JULY.
AUGUST.
SEPTEMBER.
OCTOBER.
NOVEMBER.
DECEMBER.
Burning Plant-bed.
Sowing the seed.
Protecting the bed with brush.
Making Hills.
Sowing Plaster & fighting flies.
Transplanting from the beds.
Laying by & topping.
THE FOLLOWING ARE SOME OF
OUR MOST POPULAR BRANDS:
"MAYO'S GENUINE U. S. NAVY"
"EGLANTINE." "IVY."
EVERY PLUG LABELLED
SQUARE CHEW
Export Tobacco in All Sizes & Colors.
Cutting & sticking.
Housing for curing.
Stripping & tying in hands.
Packing for market.
The above scenes are true representations of Tobacco Culture, requiring Twelve Months to complete the crop. This CALENDAR and EACH SCENE has been REGISTERED in the UNITED STATES PATENT OFFICE. All persons are cautioned not to use or copy any ONE OF THEM under penalties of the law. P. H. MAYO & BROTHER, Proprs.

Richmond and Tobacco

Figure 1
Before and after the Civil War Richmond was a market center for bright leaf tobacco grown in the southwestern parts of Piedmont Virginia.

The demand for less expensive tobacco for the British elite, who had been importing from the Spanish-American colonies, led to initial exports from Virginia of a harsh, indigenous tobacco. In 1611 John Rolfe, perhaps more famous as Pocahontas's husband than as the financial savior of the first English-American colony, obtained some seeds of the milder Spanish tobacco. The small yield from the experimental crop arrived in London in July 1613 and the future of Virginia was secured. The new tobacco strain *nicotonia tobacum* became the staple of a one-crop economy until the 1780s, when crop rotation brought in wheat and clover to revive depleted tobacco fields.

In spite of early 17th-century warnings from King James I about the instability of an entire economy based on smoke, and from King Charles I, who tried to regulate planting of the crop, overproduction was an early problem for the colonists. The situation was exploited by London merchants who took advantage of the glutted market. Throughout the period up to the American Revolution, trade imbalance grew as small planters were unable to pay debts to London merchants for imported clothes, tools, and other necessities. Not until 1802 were these

Figure 2, Plate 1
Peter H. Mayo (1836-1920) successfully revived his tobacco factory after the war in spite of labor difficulties.

Figure 3
Smoked by Generals Sherman and Grant, cigars became popular after the Civil War. The manufacture of cigars, cut plug, and pipe tobacco helped Richmond recover from the economic disasters of the war.

colonial debts repaid through a compromise plan developed in the Treaty of Paris of 1783.

Tobacco farming was the most labor-intensive of all agricultural crops in Virginia. Only as slave labor became increasingly available after the 1690s were early planters in the Tidewater regions able to grow more than one or two acres of tobacco. Tobacco fields wore out after three or four plantings, and diversification was not encouraged in the one-crop economy of Virginia. By the 19th century, therefore, in search of fresh fields, the majority of tobacco farmers had moved westerly to the Piedmont, between the fall line and the Appalachian Mountains, where a milder leaf was cultivated. The trend away from snuff, made from fire-cured tobacco, to pipe smoking called for this less harsh-tasting and brighter leaf, which was grown in both Virginia and North Carolina.

Competition from another market was new to Virginia, and the 19th-century agricultural reformers warned about the financial risks that accompanied staple crop production. Among these critics was Thomas Jefferson, who called the tobacco culture one of "infinite wretchedness. Those employed in it are in a continual state of ex-ertion beyond the power of nature to support. Little food of any kind is raised by them; so that the men and animals on these farms are illy fed; and the earth is rapidly impoverished."[1]

In 1834 Edmund Ruffin, editor of the *Farmers' Register*, sided with those concerned that neither tobacco nor

[1] Joseph Clarke Robert, *The Tobacco Kingdom, Plantation, Market, and Factory in Virginia and North Carolina, 1800-1860* (Durham, North Carolina; Duke University Press, 1938), 25.

Figures 4,5, Plate 2
By the 1870s the cigarette was challenging the cigar for popularity in an elite market. Richmond's Allen & Ginter Company attracted national attention for using female labor to hand-roll cigarettes for customers all over the world.

cotton planters ever got any leisure time. As the anti-slavery issue entered public discourse, the tobacco culture was linked to its dependence on the "peculiar institution." C.W. Gooch of Henrico County wrote in an essay, "of all the causes which have produced the present dilapidated appearance of Virginia, and prevented agricultural improvements the most operative have been the cultivation of tobacco and the existence of slavery — I mean *Negro* slavery in contradiction to *white* slavery," a term used by pro-slavery factions to describe the conditions of Northern and English factory workers.[2]

In the 1820s yet another strain of leaf that had both a mild taste and could be grown in the southwestern Virginia counties was discovered, along with an improved curing method that directed heat from an outside source through flues into the drying barn. These developments led to the popularity of flue-cured, bright leaf tobacco, which was grown in a 150-mile area of the Virginia/North Carolina Piedmont. Increased bright leaf tobacco production in the west called for improved transportation to the markets, the largest of which in the 1830s were Petersburg, Lynchburg, and Richmond. The James River and Kanawha Canal linked Richmond to Lynchburg by 1840, and by the late 1850s the state railroad network connected the capital with the rest of the state. By the time of the Civil War, Virginia produced 56 percent of the nation's tobacco goods, and Richmond's more than 50 tobacco processing factories had earned it the name "Tobacco City." (Figures 1,2)

During the war years, Virginia's tobacco fields became battlefields. Continuing domestic and foreign demand for highly prized "Virginia" tobacco had to be met by midwestern products, particularly burley from Kentucky. Cigars, smoked by both Generals Grant and Sherman, were popular during and after the war, and this spurred the growing demand for flue-cured bright leaf from Southside Virginia and areas near Durham, North Carolina. (Figure 3)

Post-bellum manufacturers refused to confront the problem of increased dependence on raw materials from outside the Richmond region, a situation that had never affected the tobacco market before 1865. Scarcity of manpower, another new dilemma, had become a production obstacle for the labor-intensive tobacco factories, which were not yet sufficiently mechanized to reduce labor needs. Without the fallback of

Figures 6,7
Several years after Allen & Ginter's rejection of the cigarette-making machine, the company was merged into the American Tobacco Company in 1890. It then began to manufacture the Fatima and Piedmont brands, formerly produced by other companies.

[2]Ibid., 28.

slavery, workers with skills or the willingness to work for low wages were hard to find. In 1870 there were only 38 tobacco factories in Richmond producing $4 million worth of goods, $1 million less than in 1860. (Figure 2, Plate 1)

As will be seen in Part II, by the 1870s Richmond led the world in the production of a new product, cigarettes, which would soon dominate the tobacco trade. As demand began to exceed the capacity of hand labor, the leading Richmond cigarette firm, Allen & Ginter, sponsored the development of a machine that would replace the mostly female workforce. (Figures 4,5) The machine was more successful than they had dared to hope. Richmond's tobacco leaders were faced with vastly increased supply and concluded that there would be no market for such a large number of "smokes." (Figures 6,7)

Such a decision was not an isolated incident in post-Civil War Richmond. The city was dominated by a profoundly conservative mood associated with the devastating defeat. Recent scholarship, such as Gaines M. Foster's *Ghosts of the Confederacy*, Michael B. Chesson's *Richmond After the War, 1865-1890*, and Christopher Silver's *Twentieth Century Richmond*, all find a conservatism that tended to isolate Richmond from the nation and even from "the New South." Foster's study of the "Lost Cause" movement sees Richmond's romanticizing of the war loss as culturally isolating. Chesson observes that resistance to technological and managerial change affected not only the once nationally dominant tobacco industry, but also the flour milling and iron processing manufactures as well. Silver follows the continuance of these trends of the 1880s into the 1960s as a conservative elite persisted in fashioning "city planning into a vehicle for maintenance of the status quo."

Figure 10

While the city missed its great chance to control a multibillion and multinational industry, the importance of tobacco to Richmond continued to grow. In the 1890s a twenty square block area along the James, "Tobacco Row," developed. (Figures 8,10) At its peak in the 1940s, Richmond produced a third of the American total, more cigarettes than any city in the world. Yet the industry was, as Chesson says, in the "economic vassalage of outside interests."[3]

The 1950s were an uneasy time for the tobacco business. In 1962 P. Lorillard left Richmond, followed by Consolidated Cigar in 1969. In 1970, Liggett & Myers vacated the old Allen & Ginter plant on Sixth and Cary Streets, which they had occupied since the dispersal of the tobacco trust in 1913. Philip Morris relocated its massive works to the suburbs in 1974. American Tobacco ceased operation in Tobacco Row in 1981 and closed its remaining non-cigarette smoking tobacco plant in May 1988. At present, therefore, only Philip Morris manufactures cigarettes in the Richmond area.

With over 11,000 workers Philip Morris remains the leading private employer in the Richmond area. Its payroll is vital to the city's economy. Philip Morris' corporate profits dwarf, however, the payroll numbers and have financed a diversification of products, such as General Foods and Kraft, that are far from tobacco and far from Richmond. (Figure 11)

The slaveowning, aggressively capitalist city of the 1850s saw its world turned upside down in 1865. The psychic shock profoundly altered the outlook of Richmond's leadership and turned them inward. Economic, political, and social decisions shaped by that pervasive conservatism produced consequences that are still powerfully felt today.

Figures 8-10
From the 1890s Richmond's tobacco manufacturing was centered in Tobacco Row, 20 square blocks along the James River. These objects came from the Whitlock Branch, at 23rd and Cary Streets. Like most Richmond tobacco factories, Whitlock was first absorbed by the American Tobacco Company; after the trust break-up in 1913, it was transferred to P. Lorillard. In the 1940s Richmond produced one-third of the total number of cigarettes produced in America.

---

[3]Michael B. Chesson, *Richmond After the War, 1865-1890* (Richmond, Virginia: Virginia State Library, 1981), 201.

Figure 11
**Philip Morris is the only company producing ciga-
rettes in Richmond today. While it is the leading
private employer, its profits from local tobacco
manufacture go toward diversification into products
other than tobacco, and far away from Richmond.**

Part II

The Modern Corporation

During a very short period in the 1880s, the new processes of production and distribution had transformed the organization of a number of major American industries — tobacco, matches, grain milling, canning, soap, and photography. These changes were revolutionary, and they were permanent. The enterprises that pioneered in adopting and integrating the ways of mass production and mass distribution became nationally known. By 1900 they were household words. Three-quarters of a century later names like American Tobacco, Diamond Match, Quaker Oats, Pillsbury Flour, Campbell Soup, Heinz, Borden, Carnation, Libby, Proctor & Gamble, and Eastman Kodak are still well known. These enterprises were similar in that they used new continuous-process machinery to produce low-priced consumer goods. Their new processes of production were so capital-intensive that production for the national and global market became concentrated in just a few plants, often only one or two. In all cases it was the massive increase in output made possible by the new continuous-process, capital-intensive machinery that caused the manufacturers to build large marketing and purchasing networks. By 1900 the names of many integrated, multi-functional enterprises had become household words. By then they were beginning to play a significant role in the transformation of the nation from what Robert Wiebe has termed a distended society of "island communities" into a far more homogeneous and integrated community.

The resulting enterprises, clustering in the food and machinery industries, were then the first industrial corporations to coordinate administratively the flow of goods on a national, indeed a global, scale. They were among the world's first modern multinationals. Their products were usually new. This was true not only for sewing, agricultural and office machinery, but also for cigarettes, matches, breakfast cereals, canned milk and soap, roll film and Kodak cameras, and even fresh meat that had been butchered a thousand miles away.

Alfred D. Chandler, *The Visible Hand: The Managerial Revolution in American Business* (Cambridge, Mass.: The Belknap Press of Harvard University, 1977).

Figures 12,13, Plate 2
In 1872, Richmond's Allen & Ginter factory began making hand-rolled cigarettes. The most skilled of Allen & Ginter's female workers could roll four to five cigarettes a minute. Soon, however, they could not keep up with the demand for the increasingly popular cigarette.

Figure 12

n the 1870s the infant cigarette industry was centered in Richmond, the marketplace for bright leaf tobacco export. John F. Allen (1814-1890) and Lewis Ginter (1824-1897) had a factory that had begun making hand-rolled cigarettes in 1872; by the 1880s it was the leading supplier for a booming national and international market. (Figures 12,13, Plate 2) These Richmond businessmen were aware that the market demand was quickly surpassing the capabilities of their mostly female hand-rollers, the most skilled of whom produced four to five cigarettes per minute. Allen & Ginter sponsored a $75,000 contest for a practical cigarette-producing machine. James Albert Bonsack's (1859-1924) 1880 invention of the cigarette-rolling machine not only altered the future of Richmond's place in the cigarette industry, but also began the transformation of that burgeoning entrepreneurial industry into a modern corporate industry. (Figures 15,16)

The machine presented to Allen & Ginter for trial use in 1881 could produce over 70,000 cigarettes in a 10-hour day. In several years the count was up to over 120,000. This continuous-process machine integrated several steps of cigarette production. "It swept the tobacco onto an 'endless tape,' compressed it into a round form, wrapped it with tape and paper, carried it to a 'covering tube' which shaped the cigarette, pasted the paper, and then cut the resulting rod

Plate 2

into the length of cigarette desired."[4] Immediate improvements included having the machine produce packaging and then insert the cigarettes into the box.

After a short trial period, Allen & Ginter decided that there would be insufficient market for mass-produced cigarettes and rejected the modern machine, whose invention, ironically, they had sponsored. In 1885 exclusive rights to the use of the Bonsack machine were acquired by James Buchanan Duke (1856-1925) of Durham, North Carolina, and the revolution in the cigarette industry began. (Figure 14)

Figure 14

In 1885 James Buchanan Duke of Durham, North Carolina acquired the rights to the Bonsack machine that Allen & Ginter had rejected. Duke quickly understood the implications of the continuous-process machine, and developed national and international purchasing, distributing, and marketing networks. Headquartered in New York City, Duke's American Tobacco Company revolutionized the cigarette industry by building a corporate structure.

The capital needed to invest in continuous-process machinery was quickly recovered through large profit increases from the rapid jump in production and decreased labor costs. Other changes, however, had to be made in purchasing and distribution to keep raw materials flowing into the continuously-operating system and to market the huge output beyond the local community. Old systems of purchasing and distribution were no longer adequate. Duke realized that he needed marketing and distribution offices in every American city in order to sell quickly the vast quantities of semi-perishable cigarettes he was producing, quantities far greater than the market of the mid-1880s actually demanded. Because the supply exceeded domestic demand, Duke also expanded into foreign markets and by 1898 was producing 1.22 billion cigarettes for sale outside the United States.

Duke established a central office in New York City, the largest distribution center in America, and staffed each of his branches with "a salaried manager, a city salesman, a traveling man to cover outlying areas, and the necessary clerical staff."[5] These middle managers, or "visible hands," were responsible for the major divisions of W. Duke and Sons, the leaf, manufacturing, and distribution departments, which purchased, cured, and shipped the raw material to the factories. Control of the complex corporation came from the New York headquarters, monitoring the flow of the product from factory to retailer via telegraphed messages from branch offices.

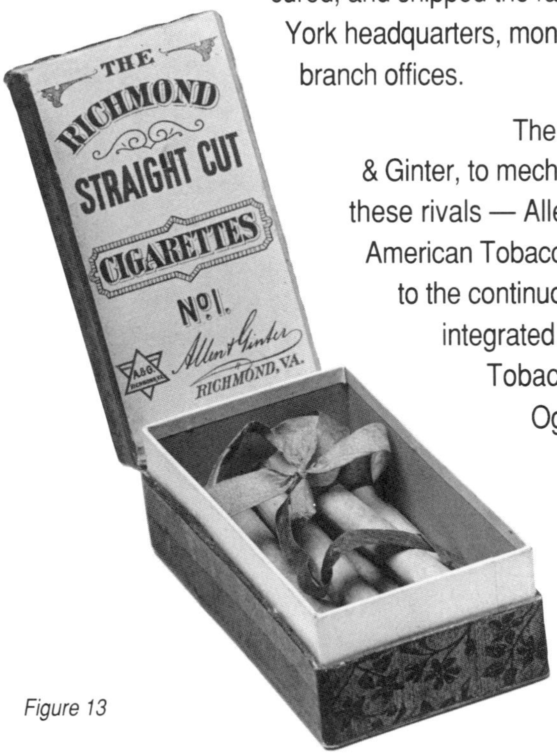

The booming cigarette demand forced Duke's three major competitors, including Allen & Ginter, to mechanize by 1887 and to build similar integrated enterprises. By the 1890 merger of these rivals — Allen & Ginter, W.S. Kimball, and Goodwin and Company of New York — into the American Tobacco Company, the price of cigarette production had declined and profits were up due to the continuous-process technology and efficient distribution coordinated through a hierarchical integrated managerial system. With subsequent takeovers of the plug-producing Continental Tobacco Company in 1898, Liggett & Myers in 1899, and the British company of Ogdens, Ltd., in 1901, Duke had pushed modern concepts of middle management to their fullest potential. On the eve of the tobacco trust break-up in 1913, British-American Tobacco Company controlled over 60 percent of the tobacco industry. The four companies that emerged after the trust was dissolved — the new American Tobacco Company, R.J. Reynolds Company, P. Lorillard, and Liggett & Myers — continued to manage their newly independent enterprises after the innovative examples set by Duke.

Figure 13

Duke's swift rise to power in the cigarette trade was not based on his technological skills or his advertising talents. He leased his machines and hired the services of advertising agencies and fulltime salaried salesmen. His success resulted from his realization that the marketing of the output of the Bonsack machine required global selling and distribution organizations. Duke became the most powerful entrepreneur in the cigarette industry because he was the first to build an integrated enterprise.[6]

---

[4] Alfred D. Chandler, Jr., *The Visible Hand, the Managerial Revolution in America* (Cambridge, Mass.: the Belknap Press of Harvard University, 1977), 250.

[5] Ibid., 383.

[6] Ibid., 382.

Figure 15

Allen & Ginter offered $75,000 for the invention of a practical cigarette-rolling machine. A model patented by a Lynchburg, Virginia, teenager, James Albert Bonsack, was adopted by Allen & Ginter on a trial basis in 1881. After a few months, the company had decided there would be no market for mass-produced cigarettes.

Figure 16

The continuous-process machine was first used in processing agricultural products. The Bonsack machine initially produced 70,000 cigarettes in a 10-hour day, and in several years over 120,000 a day. This required a constant supply of raw materials. New methods of purchasing and distribution were also necessary because of the large quantities of semi-perishable cigarettes produced.

Part III

The Creation of the American Mass Market

The advertising industry took as its mission the stimulation of consumption and the creation of new wants by quickening public appetite for alluring accoutrements of the Good Life. As movies and radio swelled into major entertainment industries, they reinforced these consumer values and aspirations. The mass culture which had first emerged in the cities was now disseminated nationwide. The result was to endow a new middle-class ideal of consumption with as much if not more authority than the genteel culture had ever been able to command.

John F. Kasson, *Amusing the Million: Coney Island at the Turn of the Century*. American Century Series. (New York: Hill and Wang, 1978.)

Figure 17

One of Duke's strategies to create a market for his huge glut of cigarettes was to use national advertising. Taking advantage of technological advances in lithography, Duke advertised in newspapers and magazines and used colorful packaging, simple brand names, and images that attracted the male smoker.

I n 1885, when James Duke contracted exclusive rights to the Bonsack machine, he intended to mass-produce cheap as well as expensive brands of cigarettes. The cigarette market of the 1870s, supplied by Allen & Ginter and other non-mechanized factories, was primarily an elite one, and the hand-rolled product catered to a very small portion of consumers. The best-selling cigarettes retailed at 10 for a nickel and 20 for a dime. Only W.T. Blackwell's Bull Durham catered to a mass audience, by providing the smoking tobacco in a muslin bag with cigarette papers, so that one could roll his own and cut down on the per unit price of the fancier pre-rolled and boxed brands. The Bonsack machine reduced the per unit cost of cigarette production to 24 cents per thousand, within reach of the average consumer. Duke now had to get the message to the masses and create a market for his glut of cigarettes. He turned to national advertising. (Figure 17)

In 1889 Duke spent $800,000 on advertising to mass market the 834 million cigarettes he had manufactured that year. By then the institution of advertising had grown from the local hyperbole of patent medicine hustlers to a national industry nurtured by what Warren Susman has called the "communications revolution."[7] In the 1850s technological progress in printing and paper-making, photography, and color lithography brought about the rapid dissemination of consumer information through daily newspapers and, later, magazines. Advertising men went from salesmen of space to a "salesmanship in print."[8] Early advertisements merely gave textual information about the product with few visual images. The potential of advertising was recognized in 1852 by New York minister Henry W. Bellows, who foresaw the ad as "a plan for letting people know what is to be had, and who has it, a scheme for creating wants by exhibiting ingenious means of supplying them, and thus developing new forms of labor and new markets for them."[9]

The creation of needs was fundamental to a society with a tradition of self-imposed austerity now experiencing new levels of mass-produced goods for purchasing. Mass production also standardized goods from fashion to soap. This democratization of commodities, distributed through mail-order catalogs and department stores, provided quantities of products, conveniently purchased, at prices that were accessible to even the working-class American. (Plate 3)

[7]Warren I. Susman, *Culture as History*, The Transformation of American Society in the Twentieth Century. (New York: Pantheon Books, 1984) xxvi.

[8]T.J. Jackson Lears, "Some Versions of Fantasy: Toward a Cultural History of American Advertising, 1880-1930," *Prospects* 9(1984), 369.

[9]Warren Susman, *Culture as History*, xxiv.

Centralized management, fixed pricing, department stores, mail order catalogs, and mass advertising weakened the relationship between salesman and buyer, client and producer, store owner and customer. Printed media provided national markets with product information that was no longer of only regional interest. Standardized goods were the same for everyone, and the printed advertisement would "sell" them. By the 1880s the advertising industry had replaced the human element that had explained product differences to the consumer in the past. For the consumer, "advertising was a form of insurance that by buying this commodity, by smoking this brand of cigarette, by driving this make of car, he would not find himself alone."[10] During the period between 1880-1920, advertising grew into the modern age with the rest of the nation's businesses. The ad man neatly shed his reputation as a hustler of sham in a kind of self-proclaimed ad campaign. By 1925 it was argued that "advertising writers compose a new chapter in civilization. It is a great responsibility to mold the daily lives of millions of our fellow men, and I am persuaded that we are second only to statesmen and editors in power for good."[11]

Tobacco advertising after the Civil War took advantage of technological advances in printing and lithography. Color lithographed broadsides and labels advertised brands of smoking and chewing tobacco and cigars throughout the century. (Figures 18-24, Plate 4) Color printing on tin had furthered the use of packaging as an advertising medium through tin tags on individual plugs and tobacco tins in all shapes and sizes. Distribution of these goods was on a local level, but in a city like Richmond, which in 1893 had over 90 tobacco factories each with a large number of brands, product differentiation was critical. In a Chamber of Commerce publication, the Cameron and Cameron firm lists the brand names of its products: five brands of "paper cigarettes," six of cheroots, five "all tobacco cigarettes," and ten more of miscellaneous blends of tobaccos. Colorful labels and packaging, along with an attention-getting brand name, therefore, were early attempts at "modern" advertising at the local level.

The lure of premiums as advertising gimmicks was already popular in the smoking tobacco and plug markets. Collecting tin tags for prizes was the forerunner of the cigarette trade card, first suggested as a use for the cardboard "stiffener" used between the two rows of cigarettes in the pack. Duke first enclosed a postage stamp series in his pre-Bonsack-machine Duke of Durham brand. Allen & Ginter also distributed picture cards, as well as premiums and coupons, all over the world in the 1870s. By the 1880s almost every brand of cigarette had color lithographed trade cards, the most popular of which bore pretty women, usually actresses, or baseball players, the new national heros. Coupons could be redeemed for small gifts ranging from college pennants to miniature oriental rugs. Trading cards as advertising ended after World War I, but those who collect them are still active today.[12] (Figures 25-30)

As improved lithographic techniques turned sheets of tin into an advertising medium, so did paper folding machines that could produce fifty small packages per minute and transform the individual cigarette package into its own advertisement. Mass production of cigarettes meant mass production of packaging to protect the semi-perishable product during distribution to retail markets. There were three kinds of cigarettes on the market — pure Turkish blend, pure domestic, and a mixture of Virginia and Turkish. The standardization of cigarettes made brand name and package design the major distinction within these categories. Allen & Ginter had used the hull-and-slide for Virginia Brights, but with very little color. Duke was the first to combine short brand names with color to create a recognizable design. By the 1920s national brands had replaced regional ones in almost all areas of domestic manufacturing, so that standard package design became a familiar part of the consumer

[10]Daniel J. Boorstin, *The Americans: The Democratic Experience* (New York: Vintage Books, 1974), 145.

[11]T.J. Jackson Lears, "From Salvation to Self-Realization," Richmond Wightman Fox and T.J. Jackson Lears, editors, *The Culture of Consumption: Critical Essays in American History, 1880-1980* (New York: Pantheon Books, 1983), 363.

[12]Harris Lewine, *Good-bye To All That* (New York: McGraw-Hill Book Company, Inc., 1970), 19-20.

culture. A 1928 publication, *Packages that Sell*, stated that the "package should be merchandized in the same way the product is merchandized."[13] By 1925, 35 percent of advertisements showed the package, up from 7 percent in 1900.

Both Duke and his rival W.T. Blackwell, who was cornering the Durham market with roll-your-own Bull Durham cigarette tobacco, recognized the cigarette's potential as a product for the masses. The standardized cigarette provided the same smoking experience for each individual, unlike the pipe or the cigar where some skill and knowledge was required for ultimate enjoyment of the product. When Duke moved his corporate headquarters to New York City, the largest urban consumer market in America, he had recognized the cigarette's convenience as something attractive to the new fast-paced existence of the urban dweller. By the 1920s the cigarette was described in a *New York Times* editorial as "Short, snappy, easily attempted, easily completed or just as easily discarded before completion—the cigarette is the symbol of a machine age in which the ultimate cogs and wheels and levers are human nerves."[14] (Figures 31,32) Like Duke, other pioneers of the new managerial revolution understood the new relationship between time, or the increasing scarcity thereof, and wage scale. Salaried managers and even wage-earning workers had new concepts of how to spend their surplus dollars. The idea that "time was money" made the quicker, but slightly more expensive cigarette more marketable to the urban consumer who had a little more money, but a lot less time. Vending machines were commonplace by the late 1920s and further proved that pack size and recognition contributed to the total convenience of cigarette smoking. (Figure 33) Selling convenience brought cigarette sales from 1.70 pounds per adult in 1918 to 5.16 in 1940. Interestingly, the roll-your-own brands continued to be popular in the rural market.

Figure 19

Figures 19-24, Plate 5

Both P. H . Mayo and Brother and Allen & Ginter used innovative advertising techniques. Mayo's roly-poly tins were unique, and Allen & Ginter's trademark, the planter, set their packaging and ad cards apart from other brands.

Figure 20

[13]Daniel J. Boorstin, *The Americans: The Democratic Experience*, 444.

[14]Michael Schudson, *Advertising, the Uneasy Persuasion — Its Dubious Impact on American Society* (New York: Basic Books, Inc., 1984), 198.

After the break-up of the tobacco trust in 1913 the major cigarette brands were divided among the four companies. The Allen & Ginter brands of Piedmont and Imperials and Cameron and Cameron's Fatima, the cheapest of the Turkish blends at 10 for five cents, were former Richmond-made brands that went to the Liggett & Myers Company. American Tobacco kept Pall Mall, Kinney Brothers' Sweet Caporal, and, of course, Lucky Strike, originally patented in 1871 by the R.A. Patterson Company in Richmond. P. Lorillard got all of the pure Turkish blends to be manufactured at the old Richmond Whitlock factory.

R.J. Reynolds Tobacco Company received no cigarette brands, and was thus forced to come up with a new marketing strategy to get into the cigarette competition, whose sales had quadrupled in recent years. Richard Joshua Reynolds (1850-1918), an early believer in advertising, spent $20,000 in 1895. On the heels of the success of Prince Albert tobacco, "the national joy smoke," Reynolds put the same formula into cigarette form. Reynolds hired the N.W. Ayer and Son Agency in 1914 and launched a $1,500,000 campaign with a four-part teaser series and a dromedary named Old Joe from the Barnum and Bailey Circus. This, the first national cigarette advertising campaign, brought with it the standardized brand, the end of regional marketing, and not incidentally made Camel the number one seller by 1919. In 1921 the "I'd walk a mile for a Camel" campaign gave Reynolds 50 percent of total national sales. (Figure 34)

Perhaps no consumer was more caught in the quandary of choices in modern life than the middle-class American woman. By the turn of the 20th century the Victorian woman had turned her domestic domain into a platform from which to catapult herself into the mainstream of the consumer culture. The increasing complexities of corporate structure left the man of the house with little time for household decisions. The man belonged to the world of production and distribution, the woman to the world of consumption. Known in the advertising trade as the "great national purchasing agent," the woman was estimated as being involved in up to 98 percent of all consumer purchases.[15] Roland Marchand observes that no relationship between advertiser and audience held as much importance as "the perception by the overwhelmingly male advertising elite that it was engaged primarily in talking to masses of women."[16] (Figures 35,36)

In the 1920s women's reaction to this new-found attention was mixed. In *Advertising, the Uneasy Persuasion* Michael Schudson suggests that the right to vote and the national exposure of women on the political scene had made women "more public people."[17] Consumption was more public as well; shopping for modern labor-saving devices for the home took place in a department store, usually at a distance from her particular neighborhood. National advertising also contributed to the more public consumption trends as one's consumer choices were no longer private, but part of a whole network of others who

Figure 21

[15]Jeffrey L. Meikle, *Twentieth Century Limited* (Philadelphia: Temple University Press, 1979), 15.

[16]Roland Marchand, *Advertising the American Dream, Making Way for Modernity, 1920-1940* (Berkeley: University of California Press, 1985), 66.

[17]Michael Schudson, *Advertising, the Uneasy Persuasion*, 182.

Figure 22

made a similar choice. T.J. Jackson Lears, on the contrary, sees women's new shopping habits, molded by "upper class male executives," as diffused answers to female demands for equality. "Feminist political claims were deflected into quests for psychic satisfaction through high-style consumption with great fanfare; as advertisers offered women the freedom to smoke Lucky Strikes they promised fake liberations through consumption."[18]

Schudson questions the degree of influence advertising actually had on the increase of women smokers in the 1920s. As late as 1924 the editor of the *United States Tobacco Journal* expressed the general opinion of the tobacco industry that women smokers were such a "novel" phenomenon that "it would not be in good taste for tobacco men as parties in interest to stir a particle toward or against a condition with whose beginnings they had nothing to do and whose end, if any, no one can foresee."[19] A 1927 article in the trade paper *Advertising & Selling*, "Why Cigarette Makers Don't Advertise to Women," explains that "the manufacturers fear that they may draw the lightning of the busybody element that brought prohibition — the long-haired men and the short-haired women whose lives are incomplete unless they are stage-managing the lives and actions of all the rest of us."[20] The 1926 Chesterfield poster portraying a couple in a romantic setting with the woman saying "Blow Some My Way" is thought to be one of the first direct suggestions that women did smoke and should be targeted in the cigarette market, just as they were in most other markets. By 1927 Marlboro, originally a cigarette designed for women, had used the back cover of a women's magazine to say "Women — when they smoke at all — quickly develop discerning taste." The ad continued, "That is why Marlboros now ride in so many limousines, attend so many bridge parties, repose in so many hand bags."[21]

Many were appalled by the advertisers' encouragement of smoking among women. In a December 18, 1929 article in *The Christian Century*, one critic lashed out at "the blatant and disgraceful advertising methods of cigarette companies in recent months.... First the woman appears in the advertisement, merely a pretty girl who becomes part of the picture; then she is offering the man a fag; next she asks

---

[18]T.J. Jackson Lears, "From Salvation to Self-Realization," 27.

[19]Michael Schudson, *Advertising, the Uneasy Persuasion*, 192.

[20]Lin Bonner, "Why Cigarette Makers Don't Advertise to Women," *Advertising & Selling* 7(October 20, 1926), 21.

[21]"Marlboro Makes A Direct Appeal," *Advertising & Selling* 8(March 23, 1927), 25.

Figure 23

Figure 24

him to blow smoke her way; finally she lights hers by his. The one encouraging thing about this development is that the grade of women pictured in the posters has distinctly deteriorated in the process, until now we see at the turn of the road the most voluptuous, greasy-haired Medusa that was ever used to advertise anything."[22]

Schudson suggests that the cigarette, associated with the young, urbane, and cosmopolitan, was a symbol that women used to separate themselves from their restricted past, and that commercialization of this independence through national advertising implied legitimacy in American society. One by one, women's colleges provided smoking rooms for the growing numbers of students who smoked. A 1937 market survey found that 95 percent of the male smokers smoked on the street, but only 28 percent thought that women should have the same privilege. In restaurants, department stores, and streetcars, the public reluctantly turned the other way as women lighted up their "torches of freedom" as a 1929 parade, sponsored by Lucky Strike, had promoted the cigarette. As one of the most democratic of commodities, the cigarette became a symbol of equality for women of the 1920s struggling for civil rights. Advertisers, however, who were primarily men, waited until the demand already existed before including women in the cigarette market, thereby sanctioning their symbol of independence.[23] (Figures 36-38)

Initial relations between advertising and David Sarnoff's "wireless music box," the radio, were uncertain. Concern existed about the potential intimacy of the contact between the radio message and the audience in their own homes. The fact that the radio could carry the message into the most private and revered American institution, the family circle, concerned advertisers. They feared that commercial messages would be seen as "an invasion of the home," and cause negative sentiment toward the industry in general. The broadcast concept — sending out messages to an unknown audience — was also looked upon with skepticism until up-to-date marketing research convinced advertisers that they could identify a particular audience.

---

[22]Joseph Clarke Robert, *The Story of Tobacco in America*, 252.

[23]Michael Schudson, *Advertising, the Uneasy Persuasion*, 185-197.

Plate 3
Improved railroad and telegraph systems also contributed to the new culture of consumption. Mail-order catalogs were one of several new ways to shop. The railroads distributed affordable, mass-produced goods to even the most remote locations.

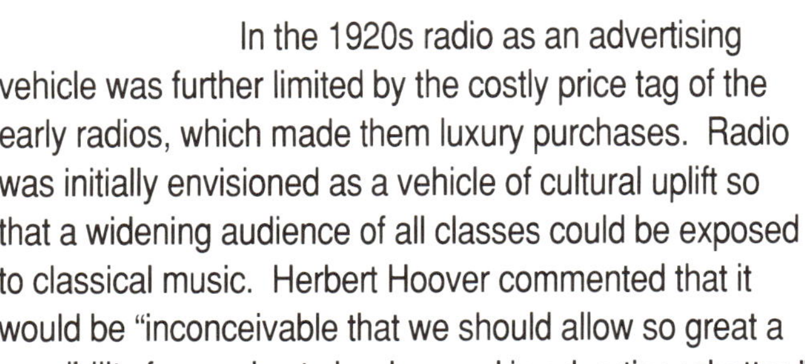

Figures 25-30

The use of premiums was an early gimmick in cigarette advertising. The cigarette trade card served as a stiffener between the rows of cigarettes. Collecting trade cards, such as baseball players, was a favorite pastime. Coupons for prizes succeeded the trade card. Only Camel brand resisted the lure of the coupon for customers.

In the 1920s radio as an advertising vehicle was further limited by the costly price tag of the early radios, which made them luxury purchases. Radio was initially envisioned as a vehicle of cultural uplift so that a widening audience of all classes could be exposed to classical music. Herbert Hoover commented that it would be "inconceivable that we should allow so great a possibility for service to be drowned in advertiser chatter."[24] Several advertisers bravely attempted to sponsor musical programs, but the lofty cultural expectations for radio were seen as tarnished by direct advertising.

Throughout the 1920s advertisers tentatively tried the radio medium. Direct advertising was still frowned upon, and in 1925 *Printers' Ink*, the advertising trade journal, warned that "advertising has no business intruding there (home) unless it is invited."[25] Ad agencies were not equipped to deal immediately with the unknown medium. Problems of technology, lack of expertise in production, and a lack of in-house announcers were other difficulties ad agencies faced during the early days of radio. Awareness of the great potential of radio marketing was combined with fear of the unknown entertainment aspects.

Saturation of the consumer market in 1928 and the depression of the 1930s forced advertisers to learn how to inject their message subtly but directly into the radio program. Even though by 1929 the owners of the $850 million worth of radios sold that year had come to expect advertisements, the protectors of the dignity of radio lamented that it had become "simply a billboard in the living room."[26] By 1940 advertisers were spending $400 million on radio advertising. Among these early radio advertising pioneers was George Washington Hill (1880-1946), a second generation executive of the American Tobacco Company.(Figure 39)

After the break-up of his American Tobacco trust, James Buchanan Duke passed the presidency of the company on to Percival S. Hill, formerly with the W.T. Blackwell firm. In 1905 Hill had brought his 25-year-old son, George Washington, into the marketing department, and the future of advertising changed forever. Young Hill's first project was the Pall Mall brand recently purchased by the trust. Hill initiated the use of the magazine back covers that traditionally carried no ads at all, as prime advertising space. By 1916 Hill had simplified the bright red-and-gold package design, and Pall Mall had reached the top of the expensive 25-cent Turkish blend market. Shortly after Duke bought Richmond's R.A Patterson Company in 1905, Hill redesigned the Lucky Strike package by making the lettering within the bull's eye more distinctive and replacing

---

[24]Roland Marchand, *Advertising the American Dream*, 89.

[25]Ibid., 40.

[26]Ibid., 108.

the "sliced plug" with "cigarettes." By January 1917, Hill had developed variations of the slogan "It's toasted" for national newspaper circulation, and the next year Lucky Strike captured 11 percent of cigarette sales. (Figure 42)

Lucky Strike was in third place in 1925 when Hill replaced his father as president of American Tobacco. After Reynolds' Camel campaign in 1913, Liggett & Myers had pushed Chesterfield into the burley-blend market's number two spot. In 1925 Hill hired pioneer ad man Albert Lasker of the Chicago firm Lord and Thomas. Twenty years earlier Lasker had developed the concept of "reason why" advertising, which "pointed advertising away from sober information and toward the therapeutic promise of a richer, fuller life."[27] The tireless Hill and Lasker, who would say of Hill "the only purpose in life to him was to wake up, to eat, and to sleep so he'd have strength to sell more Lucky Strikes,"[28] were undaunted by warnings about the risks of approaching the women's market or the sanctity of radio. Their first direct entrance into the untapped potential of women smokers was to get famous women to testify that they smoked Lucky Strike; these testimonials included actresses, opera singers, and even Amelia Earhart, who later admitted that she smoked no brand of cigarette but that her crew members did smoke Luckies. (Figure 40) These testimonials were a favorite gimmick throughout the 1930s even though the Federal Trade Commission in 1930 had prohibited endorsements by celebrities who had never used the product.

After Camels the second most important cigarette advertising campaign was launched by Lasker and Hill in 1928. By 1930 "Reach for a Lucky instead of a sweet!" had not only outraged the candy industry, but had made Lucky Strike the number one cigarette. Variations on this theme continued after the Federal Trade Commission warned that cigarettes could not be advertised as weight loss devices. "We do not say smoking Luckies reduces flesh. We do say that when tempted to over-indulge, 'Reach for a Lucky instead.'"[29] (Figure 41) Only Chesterfield, with its 1931 revival of the "Blow Some My Way" headline, and Marlboro, with ads in upper-class magazines, challenged Hill and Lasker in the women's market, but the two men continued to

[27]T.J. Jackson Lears, "From Salvation to Self-Realization," 18.

[28]Stephen Russell Fox, *The Mirror Makers: A History of American Advertising and its Creators* (New York: William Morrow and Company, Inc. 1984), 115.

[29]Harris Lewine, *Good-bye To All That*, 63.

Figure 28

Figure 29

dominate the print media with their direct advertising techniques. (Figures 42-44)

Not limited to print, Hill took his "Lucky instead of a sweet" commercial to radio. "The Lucky Strike Dance Orchestra Show" aired in September 1928 on NBC over 39 networks, and sales went up 47 percent in November and December. Brown and Williamson of Louisville, Kentucky aired "The Sir Walter Raleigh Revue," with the theme song "Rawlly Round Sir Walter Raleigh"! The days of subtle messages in radio were evidently over since the sponsors managed to mention the name of the Brown and Williamson product 70 times during the one-hour program. "Competing with essentially identical products in a lucrative market brought their aggressive selling styles to radio, pushing it to allow more overt commercials."[30]

The culture of abundance tightened its hold on America during the prosperous 1920s. Advertisers promised success and progress with the purchase of a particular product. The American consumer was represented in a 1925 *Life Magazine* by "Andy Consumer," who observed "Every advertisement is an advertisement for success. I guess that one reason there is so much success in America is because there is so much advertising."[31] Beginning with the recession of 1927 and the stock market crash in 1929, however, the 40-year-old road to success through techno-logical progress and improved business tactics had reached an apparent dead end. The economic security created by the production/distribution system was threatened and with it, the mass consumption of these goods by poverty-stricken Americans.

From 1925 to 1932 net income from manufacturing in the United States fell by more than two-thirds. Recovery began in 1933, but income did not approach the pre-Depression level until 1937.[32] Experiencing lower sales, the cigarette manufacturers' answer to the Depression economy was to drop the retail price, a reflection of lower prices of the flue-cured leaf. They also stepped up radio advertising and associated their product with popular orchestras, for example "The Camel Caravan" with Benny Goodman or Lucky Strike with the Eddy Duchin sound. In 1933 the Philip Morris bellhop came to life on the radio with the "perfect B-flat vocal cords" of Johnny Roventini, and Johnny was heard throughout the 1940s and 1950s; he officially retired in 1974. (Figures 46,47)

Figure 30

---

[30]Stephen Russell Fox, *The Mirror Makers*, 155.

[31]Roland Marchand, *Advertising the American Dream*, 285.

[32]Jeffrey L. Meikle, *Twentieth Century Limited*, 68.

Ad man Earnest Elmo Calkins, of the New York agency Calkins and Holden, came up with a solution to problems of the Depression that he saw as an issue of underconsumption due to poor methods of distribution. Calkins argued that businesses had lost touch with what the consumer really wanted; what was being manufactured did not meet the desires of the buyers, did not satisfy their fickle and ever-changing need for novelty. Calkins divided goods into "those we use" and "those we use up." He promoted the concept of a consumption engineer, who would "help us use up the kind of goods we now merely use."

This would be implemented through the *redesigning* of standardized products, which would create "artificial obsolescence." A consumer could not be stylish without the new design and would be forced to update his old purchases. Through consumer engineering the manufacturer would learn directly from the buyer what style was desired, and through the design of the product and its packaging could differentiate his product from all competitive brands. The creation of new needs to stimulate consumption would bring American industry out of the Depression. "Artificial obsolescence" through industrial design would teach Americans new consuming habits and eliminate "the obstacles in the way of the free flow of goods from factories to consumers." By the 1940s the advertising industry, through its perfected skills of creating needs in American society, had not only re-educated the consumer, but had bolstered the burgeoning field of industrial design.[33]

While cigarettes were a commodity that were "used up," "artifical obsolescence" was a potential strategy in the battle for consumer brand change that was always raging, particularly in the shrinking market of the 1930s. Lucky Strike was particularly interested in modernity and industrial design. The American Tobacco building at the 1939 New York

Figures 31-32

While the images on packaging and trade cards were directed at the male smoker, cigarette smoking was at first considered a less masculine activity than cigar or pipe smoking. The World War I doughboys' approval of cigarettes in their rations gave cigarette smoking a patriotic endorsement.

[33]Ibid., 68-73.

Figure 33
The cigarette became increasingly attractive in the fast paced urban market. Vending machines, commonplace by the 1920s, provided quick and convenient access to cigarettes.

World's Fair, one of American's first looks at the modern age, was an example of streamlining, the popular design concept of futuristic industrial efficiency. (Figure 44) Inside the building, modern technology produced Lucky Strike packages, recently redesigned by industrial designer Raymond Loewy. A souvenir book, *The Story of Lucky Strike*, described the conveyer belts of the operation as an "express highway." Speed and a new modern look would attract Depression-worn Americans to switch to Luckies. Modern design in cigarettes meant a longer "king-size" version. American Tobacco's Pall Mall and Viceroy from Brown and Williamson were the earliest versions of the streamlined product. By 1951 all of the major competitors had a king-size version along with the regular, and by 1953 "kings" had captured 25 percent of the market.[34]

World War II brought many famous smoking slogans. Cigarettes, as in the first world war, were exported to the boys overseas. "Lucky Strike Green Has Gone To War," in 1942, explained that the green pack had been replaced by a white one to save copper. The slogan was only used on the radio and rectangular cardboard carton inserts, but it was reported that enough copper was saved to provide bronze for 400 light tanks.[35] (Figure 45) Actually there never really was a shortage of green pigment, which was never used a war camouflage. The war was used an excuse to change the dark green pack to white to attract women smokers.

The longest-lasting ad headline of the forties was George Washington Hill's "Lucky Strike Means Fine Tobacco," originally the title of illustrations that promoted patriotic nostalgia by some of America's WPA artists, including Thomas Hart Benton. By 1944 the words "L.S./M.F.T" were so well known that they appeared on the bottom of every pack of Lucky Strike. Hill continued to use radio to its limits by sponsoring Kay Kyser's "College of Musical Knowledge" and the "Lucky Strike Hit Parade." Lucky Strike, Camel, and Chesterfield

---

[34]Harris Lewine, *Good-bye To All That*, 120.

[35]*Sold American! The First Fifty Years* (New York: The American Tobacco Company, 1954), 94.

dominated the market into the 50s — the era of the filter wars and television.

Daniel Boorstin in *The Americans: The Democratic Experience* marveled at the comparison between the printing press when "500 years were required to democratize learning" and the television that "with dizzying speed had democratized experience."[36] Television provided an immediate experience for Americans, who could at once share the same event with other viewers, while remaining isolated and housebound gathered around the TV set. Just as the technological advances of the railroad, telegraph, telephone, and radio had brought America together nationally, they also had whittled away at the traditional senses of community by making it unnecessary to experience news events or forms of entertainment directly with other people. To an even greater extent, varying tastes of viewers eventually made it necessary for individuals to have their own personal experience with their own personal television.

Of further concern for advertisers was the tendency of Americans to have the radio or television on, without really listening to it or without seeing it. Because interacting with the machine was fundamentally a one-way venture, the viewer became increasingly passive and the noise of the set in the room was just as comforting as what was actually being said. Perhaps television, creator of the instant image, propelled Americans full-tilt into the modern age, as defined by Susan Sontag in *On Photography*:

A society becomes 'modern' when one of its chief activities is producing and consuming images, when images that have extraordinary powers to determine our demands upon reality and are themselves coveted substitutes for first hand experience, become indispensable to the health of the economy, the stability of the polity, and the pursuit of private happiness.[37]

Transition from radio to television saw more diverse programming that enabled advertisers to reach a more diverse audience. Many of the entertainment shows and comedies, such as Lucky Strike's "Your Hit Parade" and Jack Benny's half-hour comedy show, kept much the same sponsorship format as in the early radio days, with the brand name in the title and several mentions of the product throughout the show. New avenues of programming could reach a specific type of viewer: the "Camel News

Figure 34

In 1914 R. J. Reynolds Tobacco Company spent $1,500,000 to launch the first national advertising campaign with these four teaser ads. By 1919 Camel was the number one national brand. In 1921, the "I'd walk a mile for a Camel" campaign secured 50 percent of total national sales.

[36]Daniel J. Boorstin, *The Americans: The Democratic Experience*, 397.

[37]Susan Sontag, *On Photography* (1977), p. 153, as quoted by Robert Westbrook, "Consuming Images," *Reviews in American History*, 16(March, 1988), 85.

ORIOLA
BRAND.
Patterson & Williams
Richmond, Va.
Lith. by A. Hoen & Co. B.

Plate 4

Many of the new choices in modern shopping were made by the woman of the house. Women became known in the advertising trades as the "great national shopping agent."

Caravan" with John Cameron Swayze, was one of the first national news programs on television; Lucky Strike began sponsoring college football games in 1947; Marlboro followed in 1956 with a National Football League telecast. Despite un-sophisticated technology, early televised cigarette commercials still linger in the memories of then-fascinated viewers: the 1948 Lucky Strike "Barn Dance"; P.Lorillard's 1950 dancing Old Gold box with a match box as a partner; Brown & Williamson's Kool penguin, for one of the first menthol brands in 1954. Conservative estimates in 1954 had television reaching an unheard-of 90 percent of the national market; by 1969 the tobacco industry was investing $273 million annually into televised commercials, "a staggering exercise in the use of TV for brand-switching."[38]

With all of the excitement of a new national advertising medium, however, it was the filter war, described by Stephen Fox in *The Mirror Makers* as "one of the most vicious running advertising dog fights in our advertising history,"[39] that obsessed the cigarette industry through the 1950s and 1960s. The December 1952 issue of *Reader's Digest* ran a story "Cancer by the Carton," which began the "cancer scare." P.Lorillard introduced the first filter product, Kent, that same year. In March, 1957, the Study Group on Smoking and Health, comprised of medical experts, confirmed the initial findings of 1953 that linked cigarette smoking to lung cancer. The initial slump in sales of the early fifties was remedied by the response of the tobacco industries with a scientifically perfected filter-tip, made from cellulose acetate, to reduce the amount of tar content in the smoke that gets directly into the lungs. (Figures 48-50) Nicotine amounts, contained in the tobacco leaf itself, were adjusted either by mixing high-grade bright leaf with

[38]Lincoln Diamant, *Television Classic Commercials, the Golden Years, 1948-1958* (New York: Hastings House Publishers, 1971), 104.

[39]Stephen Russell Fox, *The Mirror Makers*, 303.

blends of a lesser quality or by putting less tobacco into the cigarette. An
investigative article on the truth in filter-tip advertising in the July 1957
Reader's Digest quoted a survey conducted by the Sloan-Kettering Institute
that 70 percent of the smokers who had switched to filter from plain-tip had
done so for "health protection."[40] At the time of the article, Kent had both the
lowest tar and nicotine content and was heralded in the next month's issue of
the *Digest* for demonstrating "what a cigarette maker can accomplish if he is
sincerely seeking an improved product rather than another advertising gimmick."[41]

 Of the 26 brands tested for the *Reader's Digest* 1957 survey,
only one, Marlboro, emerged as the ultimate winner of the filter-tip advertising
war. Produced by Philip Morris and Company, Ltd., Marlboro was not a new
brand, but had been marketed from 1924 to 1954 as a woman's cigarette.
Catering to the well-to-do woman, Marlboro was advertised in magazines
such as *Town and Country*. In the 1930s it featured the "ivory tip" and the red
"beauty tip," which would hide lipstick smears on the smooth paper tip added
to prevent the cigarette paper from sticking to the lips. Only during World War
II, when the popular brands Lucky Strike, Camel, Chesterfield and Old Gold
had been shipped off to G.I.s, did Marlboro enjoy a brief surge in sales, which
immediately dropped to one-quarter of one percent of the post-war domestic
market.[42]

In 1954 Philip Morris had not yet joined the filter-tip response to the cancer

Figures 36-38
**As the cigarette became associated with the
young, with urban culture, and with the fast
pace of modern living, it was socially sanc-
tioned for men only. By the late 1920s,
however, Marlboro and Lucky Strike were
targeting the female smoker, who was still
not allowed to smoke on the street.**

[40]Lois Mattox Miller and James Monahan, "The Facts Behind Filter-Tip Cigarettes," *The Reader's Digest* 71(July, 1957), 34.

[41]Lois Mattox Miller and James Monahan, "Wanted — and Available — Filter-Tips That Really Filter," *The Reader's Digest* 72(August, 1957), 46.

[42]Scott Ellsworth, "Inventing Marlboro: A Historical Context," *Marlboro Oral History Project* (Washington, D.C.: National Museum of American History, 1986), 7,8.

warnings of the year before. The early leader of the filter-tip competition was Reynolds' Winston, introduced in March 1954 and on top by 1956. After a marketing survey of the Dallas/Fort Worth area, Philip Morris decided to re-distribute Marlboro with a filter-tip, in a new cardboard "flip top" box, the first significant change in packaging since the soft pack of 38 years before. (Figure 55) More importantly, with the help of the Leo Burnett Advertising Agency of Chicago, the image of the cigarette was to be completely changed from a feminine one in a white box with flowery script, to a bright red masculine pack. A cowboy smoking a filter-tip cigarette heretofore considered "sissy" and tasteless by smokers used to plain tips, promised that Marlboro "Delivers the goods on flavor," at the end of a day on the trail.[43] The cowboy Marlboro man, who appeared in the first ad in 1955, was designed to cater to the initial Western test market. Subsequent cam-

paigns featured men with a tattoo on their wrists. Masculine pastimes such as hunting, archery, diving, car maintenance, farming, and sports concluded with the tattooed smoker "settling back" in TV commercials from 1955 to 1957. All of these ads reassured the American male, and his woman, that smoking filters combined "old fashioned flavor in a new way to smoke." By 1958 Marlboro sales had improved to 4.5 percent of the market, but leveled off in the 1960s. The tattooed "regular guy" was replaced with male celebrities and singer Julie London, who reminded the consumers that they "got a lot to like with a Marlboro."

The new Marlboro was manufactured in Philip Morris' Richmond, Virginia plant. Before accepting the account in 1955, Leo Burnett had visited the factory. "Excepting a bakery, we had never seen a place that looked so clean or smelled so good. We were equally impressed by the research laboratories. Here we found a large staff of doctors. . .using an amazing lot of scientific equipment to analyze tobacco, filters, and smoke itself." To Burnett, therefore, Richmond, Virginia and Wirt Hatcher, who had been in the tobacco business for 44 years and was in charge of what was to be known as the "Richmond recipe," were integral parts

Figures 40,41
Hill and Albert Lasker of the Chicago firm Lord and Thomas continued to be aggressive in their Lucky Strike advertising into the 1930s. Their testimonials and direct entrance into the taboo women's market made them advertising pioneers.

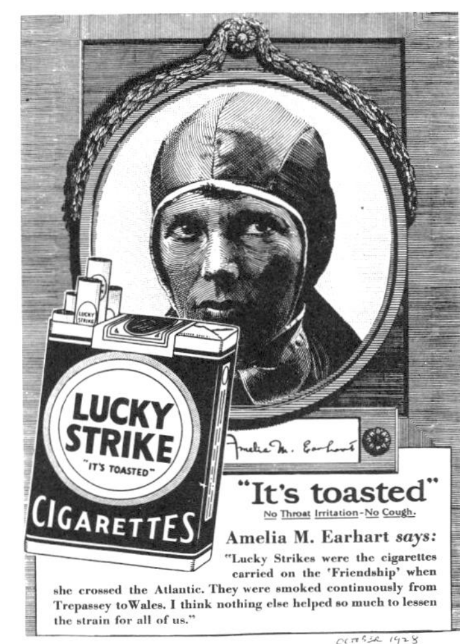

Figure 39
George Washington Hill joined the marketing department of the American Tobacco Company in 1905 and throughout his life influenced the future of advertising. Beginning with package design and magazine advertising, Hill went on to shock many with his direct advertising techniques on the radio.

Figure 42

The Lucky Strike "bulls eye" was initially the trademark of a brand of sliced plug manufactured in 1871 by the R.A. Patterson Company of Richmond. In 1905 Duke bought the company, and Hill redesigned the package. The Lucky Strike package has taken many shapes since 1871.

Figure 43

Figure 44
The field of industrial design developed out of the Depression economy. Redesigning standardized products would create artificial obsolescence, or the need to update old purchases now out of style. Hill was alert to the appeal of modernity and interested in industrial design. His Lucky Strike pavilion at the 1939 New York World's Fair was a model of the streamlined design, and he commissioned industrial designer Raymond Loewy to redesign the Luckies package.

of the new Marlboro image. In 1962, after a brief campaign stressing what Hatcher called the "better makin's" of the Richmond recipe, Burnett revived the cowboy and put him in "Marlboro Country," where he was to stay. (Figure 54) From 1962 to the present, Richmond and Marlboro Country have been entwined against a background of western scenery and rugged cowboys riding to Elmer Bernstein's musical score from "The Magnificent Seven." In 1975 for the first time Marlboro passed Winston in the domestic filter cigarette market, and in 1985 had 22.3 percent of the market. Richmond's economic prosperity bloomed alongside the international popularity of the Marlboro man.[44]

Figure 45
This famous slogan originated in 1942 with the desire to change the traditional green Lucky Strike package design to white, to attract women smokers. Heard only on the radio and printed on cardboard carton inserts, it was claimed that enough copper had been saved by eliminating the green color to provide bronze for 400 tanks! There actually was never a shortage.

In 1964, one year after the debut of "Marlboro Country," the U.S. Surgeon General's report was issued. Tobacco companies were forced by the Federal Trade Commission to establish a Cigarette Advertising Code to discourage pitches to young people as well as suggestions that smoking can improve one's health or sex appeal. At first compliance was not mandatory. In the same year the *New Yorker* was the first magazine to ban tobacco advertisements. In 1966 the Federal Cigarette Labeling Act required health warning labels on all cigarette packs. In March 1970 Congress banned cigarette advertising on radio and television to begin — ironically — on Super Bowl Sunday, one of the largest advertising sports events of the year, in January 1971. (Figures 51-53)

Stephen Fox examines the effects of these bans in light of the cultural climate of the 60s. Since most advertising was directed at women and housewives, as it had been for 40 years, this became a point of concern for the newly articulate feminist movement. The 1960s also witnessed the beginning of Ralph Nader's advocacy of consumer protection, which naturally included advertising reform. Fox concludes that like most social reform movements, the senders and recipients of the messages were the educated and sophisticated echelons of society, not the working classes who may have needed the information the most. Immediately after the TV ban, in spite of the new restrictions, cigarette sales reached new records through print advertising, billboards, and the sponsorship of sporting

[44]Ibid., 11.

Figures 46,47

During the Depression, cigarette companies increased their radio advertising. Philip Morris's bellhop, Johnny Roventini, began his radio career of calling for Philip Morris in 1933.

Figures 48-50

The excitement of the new advertising medium, television, was clouded by the cancer scare of 1952 and the resulting war between filter-tip brands of cigarettes. P. Lorillard's Kent was the first to be introduced. By 1956 the filter war was being won by Winston, an R. J. Reynolds brand.

and cultural events.[45] The foreign markets, particularly Asian and Latin American, are quickly becoming the marketplaces of the future. (Figures 57,58)

Three years after the Cigarette Advertising Code stated that models under the age of 25, athletes, or athletic events could not be pictured in cigarette ads, *Printers' Ink* ran an article that concluded, "In general cigarette advertising can be typified as groping to discover new ways of displaying and selling the brands." The article had begun by observing that the former "sexy, youthful appeals to attract a sexy, youthful market" had been replaced with "pretty bland" campaigns that focused on the "taste" of the product. The charcoal filter had been added to the list of preventative health measures taken by the cigarette manufacturers, but the consumer needed to be warned that it tasted "differently."[46] This was several years **before** the TV ban, and advertisers were already at a loss as to how to proceed, if they were to respect the new code of not targeting children or associating smoking with social and sexual success.

An article by G.A. Fine, "The Psychology of Cigarette Advertising," studied the status of cigarette print ads in 1972, one year after the ban, by surveying seven magazines, including *TV Guide*, *Playboy*, *Family Circle*, *Newsweek*, and *Psychology Today*. Twenty-seven separate name brands of cigarettes were represented, and within these were regulars, lights, 100s, etc. The author's conclusions, published in 1974, can apply to today's cigarette advertising and current questions as to the extent advertisements actually shape the actions of the consumer. "Several advertising themes are apparent: The Tar Derby, Modern Science, Humorous Relief, Masculinity, Femininity, and The Good Life. Each of these approaches (which occasionally are combined in a single ad campaign) touch upon our lives — and can perhaps be said to shape our attitudes — even for those who never have nor ever would light a cigarette. Each theme appeals to our needs, fears, and hopes — and each attempts to override the cognition of potential harm."[47]

A more recent study was conducted by researchers in the departments of medicine and communication at Stanford University. In searching through cigarette ads in magazines ranging from *Rolling Stone* and *Mademoiselle*, to *Popular Science*, from 1960-1985, they sought to prove three hypotheses: (1) since 1960 all cigarette ads, especially those in women's and youth magazines, have tended to deemphasize the activity of smoking, either by the lack of visible smoke or the absence of cigarettes at all in the image; (Figure 56) (2) emphasis has been placed on cigarettes' tar and nicotine content to suggest "safe" and "healthy" cigarettes; and (3) an in-

---

[45]Stephen Russell Fox, *The Mirror Makers*, 305.

[46]Robert H. Brown, "Cigarette Ads: Accent on 'Taste'," *Printers' Ink*, 289 (December 18-25, 1964), 27.

[47]Gary Alan Fine, "The Psychology of Cigarette Advertising," *The Journal of Popular Culture* 8 (Winter, 1974), 516.

creased association of smoking cigarettes with vitality and enjoyment of life.[48] They found that emphasis on the act of smoking decreased, while that on health and vitality through smoking increased. Even in light of these empirical findings, however, the researchers admit, "our data cannot directly link this differential focus to smoking in these groups."[49] Examination of the ads, therefore, does not necessarily address the reaction of the reader or influence on his consumer habits.

In the introduction to *Advertising, the Uneasy Persuasion*, sociologist Michael Schudson lists four roles that the "institution of abundance" plays in society: it markets consumer goods; makes commercials and advertisements; presents an omnipresent system of symbols; and serves as propaganda for a consumer culture. These four missions are not far from the 1852 comments on advertisements made by Rev. Bellows. Schudson questions whether advertisements are a "true mirror of life, a sort of fossil of history," as had been expressed in an 1897 issue of *Harper's Weekly*.[50] He suggests that advertisements show a life that would be worth emulating, but not life as it actually is. The abstract images of the advertisement connect the buyer to an entire network of other buyers; the message of the words and pictures is easily understood and available to all consumers, but conceived for no one specifically.[51] Consumers accept the images of an improved way of life with the purchase of the product, but do not necessarily believe that this image is reality. Schudson observes that the meaning intended by the advertisers is not always the one actually received by the consumer. Thus advertising reflects the tension between life as it really is and life as it is pictured in the symbols of the advertisement. After a survey of 180,000 advertisements from the 1920s and 1930s, Roland Marchand echoes this hesitation to assume that advertisements mirror historical reality or popular sentiments:

> *We may not be able to prove the specific effect of an advertisement on its readers, but neither can we prove the effect of religious tracts, social manifestos, commemorative addresses, and political campaign speeches on their audiences. . .audiences merely share the characteristics of many other suspect forms of evidence about popular attitudes: we do not know*

Figures 51-53
The anti-smoking movement has been an unwelcome undercurrent of the cigarette industry since the early 20th century. The 1964 U.S. Surgeon General's Report formalized concerns about smoking and health, and culminated in the 1971 ban on radio/TV advertising. In the 1980s smokers began to organize to promote their position of free choice.

---

[48]David Altman, Michael D. Slater, Cheryl L. Albright, and Nathan Maccoby, "How an Unhealthy Product is Sold: Cigarette Advertising in Magazines, 1960-1985," *Journal of Communication* 37(Autumn, 1987), 97.

[49]Ibid., 104.

[50]T.J.Jackson Lears, "Some Versions of Fantasy," 349.

[51]Michael Schudson, *Advertising, the Uneasy Persuasion*, 210.

exactly why they were popular or successful; we do not know if the audiences shared or adopted the ideas presented; and we have reasons to suspect that the authors had motives and biases that did not completely coincide with those of the audience.[52]

On the one hand the advertising business in the United States appears to be in a state of decline due to the division of the marketplace by an increasing number of advertising media. Competition from cable networks, ads on video tapes and other advertising directed at a specific market niche threatens the security of the early television which reached 90 percent of the market. The advertising industry continues, however, to change and respond to new market demands. As the world becomes a global village, marketing strategies must become less specialized than the former multinational taste differences. In a recent article in *The New York Times* Hamish Maxwell, chairman and chief executive of the Philip Morris Companies, commented on the challenges advertisers face in the present global market.

In country after country we are seeing the emergence of a middle-class consumer life style not unlike the one that began developing in North America a century ago. We are seeing that many tastes cross cultures, among them the simple tastes for comfort, convenience and time. . .And as tastes become global, products are bound to follow.[53]

Telecommunications has created a global village. Thus the charge to advertisers is to sell the global product.

Figures 54,55
In 1954 Philip Morris had not yet joined the filter-tip competition. Marketed from 1924 to 1954 as a woman's cigarette, Marlboro was repackaged and redistributed as a filter-tip cigarette in a red flip-top box. The Marlboro man campaign ran from 1955 to 1957. The "Marlboro Country" cowboy rode into American life in 1962, and by 1975 Marlboro had surpassed Winston in the domestic filter war.

Figure 56
Advertisements that de-emphasize the activity of smoking, or "low-involvement" ads, are not a recent technique. A 1926 example associated a mountain range with Chesterfield's constant high standards in much the same way that this now famous Salem ice cube signified cooler taste without showing smoke or a cigarette.

Figures 57,58
The ban on broadcasting cigarette advertisements did not silence the advertising industry. Print advertising, billboards, sponsorship of sporting events, promotional material, and new foreign markets, particularly in Asian and Latin American countries, boosted cigarette sales to new heights.

---

[52]Roland Marchand, *Advertising, the American Dream*, xviii.

[53]Isadore Barmash, "Strategies That Sell Everywhere," *The New York Times*, 6(October 24, 1989), D21.

Part IV

Transforming American Values

Not only the pressures but even the very abundance of the industrial economy posed problems for the maintenance of traditional social controls. At the very time Coney Island's amusement parks were attracting greatest attention, the economist and social theorist Simon Patten announced a "new basis of civilization." Industrial society, he contended, had moved from a "pain economy," in which abundance was potentially available to all. In making this declaration, Patten saw reason for concern as well as celebration. Scarcity had constituted the basic support of traditional moral prohibitions. People avoided the sins of intemperance for fear of misery. In an age of abundance, what restraints were to be put in scarcity's place: What would protect society from debauch?

At the turn of the century the nation was beginning a pivotal transition from an economy organized around production to one organized around consumption and leisure as well. Many of the values preached by genteel reformers and propagated by capitalist employers in the nineteenth century — hard work, punctuality, thrift, sobriety, self-control — were geared to the need for productivity. However, as the mass production of commodities created increasing abundance, it required an expanded mass market to absorb them. The period of Coney Island's heyday before the First World War saw the beginnings of an effort to develop that market and the increased application of technology to leisure-time pursuits. Phenomena as apparently diverse as mail-order catalogues, Model T Fords, movie serials, and mechanized amusement rides all were designed to enlarge merchandisers' and entertainers' clientele by selling to the vast multitude and amusing millions.

In this changed social setting, the old genteel injunctions lost their force. The rewards promised for those who conformed to such strictures — upward mobility, family security, social respectability — grew less compelling as new agencies emerged that offered far more immediate gratification. . . [they] prospered not by promising the attainment of ultimate rewards but by providing instant pleasures and momentary release from work demands and social prescriptions.

John F. Kasson, *Amusing the Million: Coney Island at the Turn of the Century* (New York: Hill and Wang, 1978).

In the post-Reconstruction years America was a loosely connected network of what Robert H. Wiebe calls "island communities," small towns clustered around an urban center, that "managed to retain the sense of living largely to themselves."[54] Citizens of these towns abided by the Protestant philosophy that hard work would bring rewards and riches. (Figure 59) Wiebe explains the non-negotiability of the work ethic: "People of very different backgrounds accommodated themselves to this Protestant code which had become so thoroughly identified with respectability, and the keepers of the national conscience applied its rules with slight margin for the deviant. . . . Their truths derived from what they knew: the economics of a family budget, the returns that came to the industrious. . .and the advantages of a wife who stayed home and kept a good house."[55] The 1870s saw the end of the producer economy, in which the small

[54]Robert H. Wiebe, *The Search for Order, 1877-1920* (New York: Hill and Wang, 1978), 2.

[55]Ibid., 4.

Plate 5

Poor RICHARD improved:

BEING AN

ALMANACK

AND

EPHEMERIS

OF THE

MOTIONS of the SUN and MOON;

THE TRUE

PLACES and ASPECTS of the PLANETS;

THE

RISING and SETTING of the SUN;

AND THE

Rifing, Setting *and* Southing *of the* Moon,

FOR THE

YEAR of our LORD 1753:

Being the Firft after LEAP-YEAR.

Containing alfo,

The Lunations, Conjunctions, Eclipfes, Judgment of the Weather, Rifing and Setting of the Planets, Length of Days and Nights, Fairs, Courts, Roads, &c. Together with ufeful Tables, chronological Obfervations, and entertaining Remarks.

Fitted to the Latitude of Forty Degrees, and a Meridian of near five Hours Weft from *London*; but may, without fenfible Error, ferve all the NORTHERN COLONIES.

By *RICHARD SAUNDERS*, Philom.

PHILADELPHIA:

Printed and Sold by B. FRANKLIN, and D. HALL.

Figure 59

The 1870s saw the end of a culture which emphasized that personal and financial rewards could be won by hard work and thrift. Mass-produced goods and the bureaucratic corporate system turned a society of savers, as advocated in Poor Richard Improved's "A penny saved is a penny earned," into a consumer culture of abundance.

business owner/artisan produced what the local market demanded; there were no problems with distribution and pricing was on the local level. To own one's business had been the goal of the American worker since the 17th century. As the bureaucratic corporate system merged with technological progress, the traditional, individual lifestyle in these communities gave way to "regulative, hierarchical needs of urban-industrial life."[56] Mass-produced goods turned the production and market-oriented economy into a consumer culture of abundance.

Telegraph technology and the railroads did more than improve industrial profits. By the 1880s the national system of railroads had corralled remote rural communities and isolated farmers into a national network. Not only did the rail carry raw materials from farms to processing plants in the cities, but the opportunities of the urban centers were only a train ride away. Exposure to the urban environment hastened the homogeneity of the American marketplace. Mandated by the railroad companies in 1883, the standardization of time zones also lessened the individualism of the rural community. Time and space, therefore, were redefined for most Americans by the arrival of the national railroad.

The mechanization of farms forced many farm laborers into the cities. These laborers and the masses of immigrants were poorly prepared for working conditions in the factories. Beyond the individual degradation of being "controlled" by a machine and a seldom seen bureaucratic management, the factory worker had to learn a whole new system of wage-earning, based not on how much one produced, but the time one spent in the factory. Time was money; regulated work time left the worker with disposable time and income. Freedom to buy the vast assortment of mass-produced, newly affordable commodities was an entirely new idea to the late 19th century worker, accustomed to the traditional philosophy of scarcity and owning only the material goods earned by his individual endeavors.

The working classes were not the only Americans wrestling with problems of rapid social changes. The bourgeoisie, many of whom belonged to an emerging bureaucratic elite, experienced anxieties which stemmed from challenges to the Protestant values of personal and national salvation through self-denial and restraint.[57] Because the by-product of an economy based on mass production was mass consumption, the moneyed classes found their values aligned against the new powers of social legitimacy through unbridled consumption. Spontaneous gratification, the motto of a consumer society, was a secular ideal and left the spiritual needs of Victorian intellectuals unsatisfied.

[56] Ibid., xiv.

[57] T.J. Jackson Lears, *No Place of Grace, Antimodernism and the Transformation of American Culture, 1880-1920* (New York: Pantheon Books, 1981), 4-58.

In his 1884 medical treatise *American Nervousness*, George Miller Beard explains that "Modern nervousness is the cry of the system struggling within its environment."[58] This anxiousness, labelled as neurasthenia, was most prevalent among the northeastern bourgeoisie, who were particularly aware of changes in the sense of selfhood, a result of the interdependency of the bureaucratic corporate structure and the anonymity of urban existence. Modern luxuries such as indoor plumbing and canned foods — what Daniel Boorstin calls "the thinner life of things"[59] — provided a sense of unreality for those used to the primary experiences of life, or dealing with nature and people on an individual basis without the intermediary conveniences of appliances or a surrounding corporate structure. By the end of the 19th century, a Northern intellectual and social elite was desperately seeking a sense of reality, a sense of self, a reconciliation between the lost Protestant framework of personal salvation and the new pressures of the therapeutic society.

T.J. Jackson Lears defines therapeutic ethos in his article "From Salvation to Self-Realization, Advertising and the Therapeutic Roots of the Consumer Culture, 1880-1930," as the fretful pre-occupation with preserving secular well-being, seeking self-realization in this world rather than salvation in the afterlife through self-denial. By the 1890s, searching for cures for the "sick society" obsessed the educated classes. The most popular remedy was "abundance therapy," which advocated finding "more life" not only through the purchasing of goods, but also leisure activities, and the development of a "vital personality."[60]

Lears intertwines this desire for external approval with the workings of the bureaucratic systems, wherein personal magnetism became the key to advancement up the corporate ladder. He calls this "impression management," another culprit in the destruction of individual selfhood.[61] The transition from self-worth based on individual character to self-esteem earned from the approval of others brought with it a rash of self-help books. Henry Laurent's *Personality: How to Build It*, 1915, distinguished character from personality: "personality is the quality of being Somebody."[62]

Early glimpses of the other-directed American, a character trait studied by David Riesman in *The Lonely Crowd*, were evident amidst the urban upper middle classes, suddenly faced with a plethora of complex choices, but with no framework of guidance. Riesman summarizes: "What is common to all the other-directed people is that their contemporaries are the source of direction for the individual, either those known to him or those with whom he is indirectly acquainted, through friends or through the mass media."[63]

Concern over ownership of particular goods was not a novelty of the late 19th century. What was new was the public realization, crossing all class lines, that what they owned could make or break their position in the community, factory, or business office. Mary Douglas in *The World of Goods, Towards an Anthropology of Consumption*, supports Riesman's other-directed theory with the overall need for people to consume in order to relate to others; goods were part of an information system. "Consumption has to be recognized as an integral part of the same social system that accounts for the drive to work, itself a part of the social need to relate to other people, and to have mediating materials for relating to them."[64]

Surrounded by a world of readily available commodities and torn between contradictory desires for spontaneous gratification and old measures of calculated self-control, the consumer of the upper and lower classes was the target for moralistic literature by contemporary social thinkers.[65] The economist Simon Nelson Patten (1852-1922) focused on the effects of the rising standard of living on the working classes. From a

[58]Alan Trachtenberg, *The Incorporation of America, Culture and Society in the Gilded Age* (New York: Hill & Wang, 1982), 47-48.

[59]Daniel J. Boorstin, *The Americans: The Democratic Experience* (New York: Vintage Books, 1974), 411.

[60]T.J. Jackson Lears, "From Salvation to Self-Realization, Advertising and the Therapeutic Roots of the Consumer Culture, 1880-1930," 4-17.

[61]Ibid., 8.

[62]Quoted in Warren I. Susman, *Culture as History, the Transformation of American Society in the Twentieth Century* (New York: Pantheon Books, 1984), 271-285.

[63]David Riesman, *The Lonely Crowd* (New Haven: Yale University Press, 1950), 21.

[64]Mary Douglas, *The World of Goods, Towards an Anthropology of Consumption*, (New York: W.W. Norton and Company, 1979), 4.

[65]Daniel Horowitz, *The Morality of Spending, Attitudes Toward the Consumer Society in America, 1875-1940*, (Baltimore: Johns Hopkins University Press, 1985), 30-41.

progressive platform of social reform, Patten's 1907 *The New Basis of Civilization* advocated a program to include the poor in the abundant society by finding the social and environmental causes of poverty and raising the masses to a new level of culture and education by using economic surplus to philanthropic ends. He recognized the plight of the immigrant cultures in factory conditions and promoted community and ethnic festivals as more "uplifting" leisure activities than amusement parks or movie theaters. He saw material emulation of the upper classes as exhausting for the workers, who worked harder in order to buy more. "More good things will not elevate like fewer bad things relieve," Patten preached in *Product and Climax*, 1909; society's rejection of over-production would lessen the burden on the workers to consume.[66]

Thorstein Veblen (1857-1929) in his much quoted *The Theory of the Leisure Class: An Economic Study in the Evolution of Institutions*, 1899, launched an attack on the wasteful consumer habits of the wealthy and the destructive results emulation had on the quality of the life of the poor. Still wrestling with the place of restraint in the culture of consumption, Veblen saw imitation of the wealthy as resulting in "conspicuous decency" rather than "physical comfort and fulfillment of life."[67] Veblen's ideal solution was "maximum production to satisfy noninvidious desires." He felt that affluence created exclusiveness and threatened the communal spirit already at risk in the city. Although he focused his criticism on the spending habits of the elite, he ultimately was no closer to bridging the gaps between the work ethic and responsible consumption of goods.

The struggle between goods as luxuries and goods as necessities continued into the World War I period. As the traditional moralities of the period before mass production continued to be threatened, in 1900 inflation began to erode the affordability of many consumer goods. In his research into family budgets from 1875-1940, Daniel Horowitz suggests that coping with inflation also changed spending habits of the middle class. "Observers believed inflation was among the forces undermining the traditional family in which the man worked in the world and the woman in the home…to many the emergence of the 'New Woman' threatened to undermine the traditional household. . .tension between spouses. . ., often resulted from fights over family budgets thrown out of kilter by escalating prices and a wide range of economic choices."[68] (Figure 61) Simon Patten in his 1913 "The Standardization of Family Life" expressed concern about the lack of family savings in middle class households. He suggested purchasing less expensive goods and concentration on savings for children's education. Horowitz chronicles the "save or spend" debate during the steady inflation between 1900-1916. "Inflation in making some middle class people worry less about savings, sacrifice, and self-control, helped them more readily accept new levels of comfort."[69] (Figure 60)

Advertisers helped too. By 1920 household advancements were no longer considered a luxury for the few, but a necessity for *any* modern household. While this was a step forward from the mindset of

[66]Quoted in ibid, 34.

[67]Quoted in ibid., 38.

[68]Ibid., 69-70.

[69]Quoted in ibid., 86

Miss Lillian Russell.
FORGET-ME-NOT:- TRUE FRIENDSHIP.
REGISTERED TRADE MARK.
Richmond
Straight Cut
No 1 Cigarettes
ARE
THE
BEST

Plate 6

denial and restraint of the 1880s, the middle-class housewife remained content with purchasing as little as she could get along with. For example, one telephone was a necessity, two or three would have been an irresponsible waste of money. Roland Marchand considered how AT&T had launched a campaign that would rid the black telephone of its reputation as a "dull necessity," and convince the American consumer that two or more phones not only would provide "comfort and convenience" but would "prevent little annoyances that destroy pleasant moods."[70]

Throughout the 1920s industrialists such as Henry Ford recognized the value of the worker as a consumer. The forty hour week and increased wages left more leisure time for the worker to spend money. ". . .Increased consumption would promote discipline in work and savings. Because people come to see luxuries as necessities, existing high standards of living will promote enterprise, energy and stability among all classes."[71]

Helen M. and Robert S. Lynd did not agree. In their 1929 critique of the deterioration of a mid western "island community," *Middletown: A Study in Modern American Culture*, the Lynds observed how consumption patterns triggered by outside forces had robbed the town and its citizens of all spontaneity. "It is perhaps impossible to overestimate the role of motion pictures, advertising, and other forms of publicity in this rise in subjective standards."[72]

The Lynds were among several intellectual moralists who hoped that each crisis of the early 20th century — World War I, the Depression, World War II — would redirect Americans' attention from mass-consumed materialism to renewed interest in individualistic and less capitalistic pursuits. However, artificial obsolescence — along with frustration from material deprivation during the Depression and war years — only fueled increased buying habits of postwar Americans.

The naiveté of the rampant consumption of the 1950s has developed into what Bush Administration budget director Richard Darman has recently called a "self-indulgent" behavior which reflects the affliction "now-now-ism." "We consume today as if there were no tomorrow. We attend too little to the issues of investment necessary to make tomorrow brighter. Like the spoiled '50s child. . .we scream on the verge of a collective now-now-scream. . . . Individuals are encouraged toward current consumption at the expense of saving and long-term gain. . . .Some people. . .trust in the motto: 'You can have it all,' others. . .live by the dictum, 'Take the money and run.'. . .Our culture seems to tolerate all this rather blithely."[73]

---

[70]Marchand, 117-119.

[71]Horowitz, 136.

[72]Quoted in ibid., 149.

[73]Peter T. Kilborn, "Darman Issues Warning on 'Self-Indulgent' U.S.," *The New York Times* 4(July 21, 1989), 1.

Changing American values enter into our culture through many avenues. A major one is advertising. The social implications of advertising and the graphics of packaging influence our daily lives. Image, a novel idea in the 1920s, is now attached to every consumer product. "Image is increasingly an important aspect of personal identity," observed Stuart Ewen, author of *Captains of Consciousness, Advertising and the Social Roots of the Consumer Culture.* "Designers need to be aware that there are certain values embedded within their imagery."[74] Again, the realities of the global village have homogenized the advertising experience into what has been called "the Americanization of the visual experience."[75] One graphic artist observed, "We are suddenly aware that there are consequences in the transmission of information, and more pressing issues than making something look good."[76]

These admonitions and observations are reminiscent of those of the social moralists of the 1880s. Long-term consequences of the one-hundred-year transformation from the 19th-century producer economy to the 1980s culture of immediate gratification have turned the United States into a debtor nation with shrinking production resources. In an "advertorial" in the October 5, 1989 issue of *The New York Times*, the Mobil Corporation expressed concern about lack of American productivity in the global market. "For over 20 years our rate of national savings has been one of the lowest in the free world. . . .Yet without savings there can be no investment in plants, capital equipment, and new technology; without such investment, there can be little or no growth in productivity."[77] The warnings of Veblen, Patten, the Lynds, and now the President's budget director make it clear that the effects and the evaluation of the revolution in American values will continue into the 21st century. ◆

[74]Patricia Leigh Brown, "Designers Worry About Self-Image," *The New York Times* 6(October 12, 1989), D23.

[75]Ibid.

[76]Ibid.

[77]The Mobil Corporation, "A Dose of Reality," *The New York Times* 6(October 5, 1989), A31.

Figure 61
The traditional values of American women were challenged by the new consumer culture. The man spent more time in the workplace, leaving the woman at home with new responsibilities.

ILLUSTRATIONS

Frontispiece
Just the Right Note, 1929.
Modern Priscilla, March, 1929.
Printed advertisement for *Camel* cigarettes.
J. Walter Thompson Company Archives,
Manuscript Division,
William R. Perkins Library.
Duke University, Durham, North Carolina.

Color Plates
Plate 1
P.H. Mayo and Bro.'s 1881 Tobacco Calendar, United States NAVY Tobacco Works, Richmond, Virginia. 1881.
Lithographed print by the A. Hoen and Company, Richmond, Virginia.
Valentine Museum.
541.14.
Plate 2
Richmond-A Cigarette Factory, 1887.
From *Harper's Weekly,* vol. 31, no. 1569, 15 January 1887.
Wood engraving.
Kym S. Rice, Washington, D.C.
Plate 3
Sears Roebuck and Co. Incorporated Cheapest Supply House on Earth/Consumers Guide/Catalogue No. 110, 1900.
Chicago Historical Society, Chicago, Illinois.
Plate 4
Oriola Brand, Patterson & Williams, Richmond, Va., c. 1880.
By A. Hoen and Company, Richmond, Virginia.
Lithograph on paper.
Valentine Museum.
Gift of Richard Duckhardt.
V52.159.10.
Plate 5
Tuxedo Tobacco. The Perfect Tobacco. Beg For It., c. 1915.
Lithograph on paper.
Museum of Tobacco Art and History/United States Tobacco Company, Nashville, Tennessee.
Plate 6
Richmond Straight Cut No. 1 Cigarettes are the Best. Miss Lillian Russell. Forget-Me-Not-True-Friendship, c. 1880.
Lithograph on cardboard.
Staples & Charles, Washington, D.C.
Plate 7
Tobacco Farmer, 1939.
Plaster figure in wooden shadow box.
The American Tobacco Company, Richmond, Virginia.

I. Richmond and Tobacco
Figure 1
Tobacco Exchange, Richmond, Virginia, by W. L. Sheppard, 1867.
Wood engraving.
From *Harper's Weekly*, vol. 11, no. 538, p. 253, 20 April 1867.
Valentine Museum.
Gift of Mrs. Wesley Wright.
V88.88.3.
Figure 2
Peter Mayo in his office, P.H. Mayo & Brother Tobacco Factory, c. 1900.
Photograph.
Agriculture Division,
National Museum of American History,
Smithsonian Institution, Washington, D.C.
Figure 3
General Grant Smoking a Cigar, c. 1880.
Clockwork mechanical toy manufactured by Ives, Blakeslee and Williams Company, Bridgeport, Connecticut.
Painted cast iron on wooden base.
The Strong Museum, Rochester, New York.
Figure 4
Lewis Ginter (1824-1897), c. 1890.
Photograph.
Valentine Museum.
54.142.3.
Figure 5
The Cigarette Manufacture at Richmond, 1883.
From *Leslie's Illustrated*, vol. 55, no. 1429, p. 420, 10 February 1883.
Wood engraving.
Valentine Museum.
45.28.584.
Figure 6
Home of Fatima Cigarettes, c. 1910.
Photograph.
Cook Collection,
Valentine Museum. 1124.
Figure 7
Wheeling out crates of Piedmont and Fatima brands from Allen & Ginter warehouse.

c. 1915.
Photograph.
Cook Collection,
Valentine Museum. 1109.
Figure 8
*Loving Cup, **Presented to P. Whitlock, Jan. 31, 1905/Affection of Employees, Whitlock Branch***, 1905.
Silver.
Valentine Museum.
Gift of Mrs. Edwin S. Hirschler.
V76.2.
Figure 9
*Two boxes for **Old Virginia Cheroots***, c. 1915.
Wood.
Philip Whitlock Klaus, Sr.
Figure 10
*Front Page of Newspaper **Richmond Making 350,000 Cigarettes Daily, In Same Time, Americans Smoke Nearly Billion***, 1948.
March 21, 1948 Richmond *Times-Dispatch*.
Valentine Museum.
V88.190.
Figure 11
Philip Morris's big Bite by L.J. Davis, 1989.
From *New York Times Magazine*, April 9, 1989.
Valentine Museum.
Gift of Jane Webb Smith.
V88.181.27.

II. Modern Corporation
Figure 12
The Cigarette Maker, Virginia Brights Cigarettes, Crop of 1884, 1884.
Photograph on advertising card.
Staples & Charles, Washington, D.C.
Figure 13
*Box of 6 hand-rolled cigarettes, **Richmond Straight Cut No. 1 Cigarettes, Allen & Ginter, Richmond***, c. 1880.
Valentine Museum.
Gift of Mrs. Tate Irvine.
V50.118.26.
Figure 14
James Buchanan Duke (1865-1925), 1900.
Engraving.
W. Duke Sons and Company Papers,
Manuscript Department,
William R. Perkins Library.
Duke University, Durham, North Carolina.
Figure 15
J.A. Bonsack Cigarette Machine. No. 238,640. Patented March 8, 1881, 1881.
Drawing on paper.
Richard Harvey Wright Papers,
Manuscript Department,
William R. Perkins Library,
Duke University, Durham, North Carolina.
Figure 16
Excelsior Cigarette Machine, No. 780, 1910.
Made in Rotterdam, Holland by J.C. Muller.
Iron.
National Tobacco Textile Museum, Danville, Virginia.

III. Advertising: Creating the American Mass Market
Figure 17
Duke's Cameo Cigarettes with little holders, 1886.
From *Puck*, no reference.
Valentine Museum.
V88.155.26.
Figure 18
Tobacco Tins, 1870-1950
Lithographed tin.
Valentine Museum.
Figure 19
*Eglantine & Ivy, **Mayo's Tobacco is Always Good***, c. 1880.
Lithographed cardboard advertising card.
Warshaw Collection of Business Americana,
Archives Center,
National Museum of American History,
Smithsonian Institution, Washington, D.C.
P.H. Mayo and Brother Incor., Mayo's Cut Plug is Always Good., Richmond, Virginia, c. 1880.
Lithographed cardboard advertising card.
Staples & Charles, Washington, D.C.
*Eglantine & Ivy. **Mayo's Tobacco is Always Good***, c. 1880.
Lithographed cardboard advertising card.
Staples & Charles, Washington, D.C.
*Eglantine & Ivy. **Mayo's Tobacco is Always Good***, c. 1880.
Lithographed cardboard advertising card.
Staples & Charles, Washington, D.C.

Figure 20
All the Rage, Alexander Cameron and Company, Richmond, Va., c. 1890.
By A. Hoen and Company, Richmond, Virginia.
Lithograph on paper.
Valentine Museum.
Gift of Richard Duckhardt.
V52.159.30.
Figure 21
Louisiana Perique Tobacco tin, c. 1900. Allen & Ginter, The American Tobacco Company.
Lithographed paper on tin.
Vlanetine Museum.
V88.150.6.
Allen & Ginter's Original Imperial Cube Cut Smoking Mixture, American Tobacco Company. c. 1910.
Lithographed paper on tin.
Valentine Museum.
V88.148.1.
The Richmond Mixture for Smoking, No. 1. Prize Medal Awarded Philadelphia 1876. Prize Medal Awarded Paris 1878.
c. 1900.
Lithographed tin.
Valentine Museum.
V88.150.6.
Allen & Ginter's Imperial Smoking Mixture Cube Cut. c. 1900
Lithographed tin.
Cassandra O. Stoddart, Richmond, Virginia.
Figure 22
Mayo's Cut Plug, 1912.
Lithograph on tin in the form of a storekeeper.
Patent design for roly-poly tin, W.I. Tuttle.
Can manufactured by Tindeco for American Tobacco Company.
Museum of Tobacco Art and History/United States Tobacco Company, Nashville, Tennessee.
Mayo's Cut Plug, 1912.
Lithograph on tin in the form of a mammy.
Patent design for roly-poly tin, W.I. Tuttle.
Can manufactured by Tindeco for American Tobacco Company.
Museum of Tobacco Art and History/United States Tobacco Company, Nashville, Tennessee.
Mayo's Cut Plug, 1912.
Lithograph on tin in the form of a man singing.
Patent design for roly-poly tin, W.I. Tuttle.
Can manufactured by Tindeco for American Tobacco Company.
Museum of Tobacco Art and History/United States Tobacco Company, Nashville, Tennessee.
Figure 23
Carton of ten packages of "Richmond Gem, Virginia and Perique, Allen & Ginter," c. 1880.
Cardboard carton with labeled tobacco packs.
Valentine Museum.
V88.149.
Figure 24
Allen & Ginter, Manufacturers of Cigarettes and Tobacco, Richmond, Virginia. U.S.A. "Richmond Gem," "Richmond Straight Cut No. 1," "Our Little Beauties" and other well known brands, 1880.
Lithograph on cardboard.
Staples & Charles, Washington, D.C.
Figure 25
Old Mill Cigarettes, Baseball Series Selection from Texas, South Atlantic Virginia, and Southern Leagues, Richmond Team, c. 1910.
Lithographed cardboard.
Valentine Museum.
Gift of Mr. Henry Wallerstein, Jr., and Mr. Edward T. Wallerstein.
56.116.4,6,8,13,19,20,23,25,28.
Figure 26
Raining in London (13), Florodora (20), Only a Mouse (21), Just From London (23), Piedmont the Cigarette of Quality, 1902.
By H. King, copyright by S. Anargyros.
Lithographed cardboard.
Valentine Museum.
Gift of Estate of Miss Frances B. Scott.
37.40.2
Figure 27
50 Fish from American Waters/Published by Allen & Ginter, Richmond, Virginia, c. 1890.
Lithograph on paper, booklet.
Valentine Museum.
Gift of Mrs. Spencer C. Devan.
63.155.6.
Figure 28
*Folding Chair, **Smoke Piedmont the Cigarette of Quality***, c. 1915.
Lithographed tin, wood.
National Tobacco Textile Museum, Danville, Virginia.

Figure 29
R.A. Patterson Lucky Strike, c. 1880.
Felt.
Warshaw Collection of Business Americana,
Archives Center,
National Museum of American History,
Smithsonian Institution, Washington, D.C.

Figure 30
An Out and Out Challenge, Compare Camels with any cigarette at any price. No Coupons-All Quality, c. 1920.
Lithograph on paper.
R.J. Reynolds Tobacco Company Archives, Winston-Salem, North Carolina.

Figure 31
Welcome Home to Your Old Job, c. 1918.
Whitlock Branch of the P.Lorillard Company, Richmond, Virginia.
Photograph.
Cook Collection,
Valentine Museum, 1095.

Figure 32
Buying Cigarettes at the Traveling Sales Store, France, 1918-1919.
Photograph.
U.S. Army Quartermaster Scrapbooks.
Library of Congress, Washington, D.C.

Figure 33
*Vending Machine, **Cigarettes***, c. 1925.
One armed bandit slot/cigarette machine.
National Tobacco Textile Museum, Danville, Virginia.

Figure 34
Camels, 1913-1916.
First of four teaser ads.
Collection of Thomas A. Gray, Winston-Salem, North Carolina.
The Camels are coming! ,1913-1916.
Second of four teaser ads.
Collection of Thomas A. Gray, Winston-Salem, North Carolina.
Camels. Tomorrow there'll be more CAMELS in this town than in all Asia and Africa combined! , 1913-1916.
Third of four teaser ads.
Collection of Thomas A. Gray, Winston-Salem, North Carolina.
Camel Cigarettes are Here! 1913-1916.
Fourth of four teaser ads.
Collection of Thomas A. Gray, Winston-Salem, North Carolina.

Figure 35
Smoke Old Virginia Cheroots/Manufactured only by The Whitlock Branch of the American Tobacco Company, Richmond, Va. U.S.A., c. 1900.
Lithograph on card.
Warshaw Collection of Business Americana,
Archives Center,
National Museum of American History,
Smithsonian Institution, Washington, D.C.
The modern woman is a wise buyer, 1931.
Printed advertisement for Kellogg's Corn Flakes in *Delineator*, September, 1931, Vol. 119, page 57.
Elizabeth W. Hopper, Richmond, Virginia.

Figure 36
Virginia Slims/You've Come a Long Way, Baby!, 1989.
Printed poster.
Valentine Museum.
Gift of Philip Morris, U.S.A.
V89.244.1.

Figure 37
Windproof Beauty/Zippo Windproof Lighters, 1940.
Printed brochure.
Valentine Museum.
V88.185.1.

Figure 38
Virginia Cigarettes, 1948.
Tin sign.
Valentine Museum.
V88.148.4.

Figure 39
George Washington Hill, (1880-1946), c. 1925.
Photograph.
The American Tobacco Company, Richmond, Virginia.

Figure 40
Amelia M. Earhart says: "Lucky Strikes were the cigarettes carried on the 'Friendship' when she crossed the Atlantic.", 1928.
The Atlantic Monthly, October 1928, p. 127.
Printed advertisement.
Warshaw Collection of Business Americana,
Archives Center,
National Museum of American History,
Smithsonian Institution, Washington, D.C.

Figure 41
Shadows Huger than the shapes that cast them. Avoid that future shadow. When Tempted Reach for a Lucky instead, c. 1930.
Printed advertisement, no reference.
Warshaw Collection of Business Americana,
Archives Center,
National Museum of American History,
Smithsonian Institution, Washington, D.C.

Figure 42
Lucky Strike/R.A. Patterson Tobacco Co., Richmond, Va., c. 1900.
Fabric pouch.
Valentine Museum.
V88.153.14.
Lucky Strike/R.A. Patterson Tobacco Co., Richmond, Va./Cut Plug,
c. 1900.
Lithographed tin.
Valentine Museum.
V88.148.2.
Lucky Strike/R.A. Patterson Tobacco Co., Richmond, Va./Cut Plug,
c. 1900.
Lithographed tin.
Valentine Museum.
V88.148.3.
Lucky Strike/R.A. Patterson Tobacco Co., Richmond, Va./Sliced Plug,
c. 1900.
Tin with lithographed paper.
Valentine Museum.
V88.152.
Lucky Strike Tobacco/Half and Half/Buckingham Bright Cut Plug Smoking Tobacco, c. 1910.
Lithographed tin.
Valentine Museum.
V88.180.9.
Lucky Strike/"It's Toasted"/Long Cut Tobacco, c. 1920.
Tin with lithographed paper.
Valentine Museum.
V88.151.
Lucky Strike/"It's Toasted"/Little Cigars, c. 1920.
Printed cardboard.
Valentine Museum.
V88.153.1.
Lucky Strike/"It's Toasted"/Cigarettes, c. 1935.
Cigarette package.
Valentine Museum.
V88.153.2.
Lucky Strike/"It's Toasted"/Flat Fifties, c. 1940.
Lithographed tin.
Valentine Museum.
V88.153.13.
Lucky Strike/"It's Toasted"/Cigarettes, c. 1945.
Cigarette package.
Valentine Museum.
V89.243.2.
Lucky Strike Cigarettes, c. 1950.
Printed cardboard carton.
The American Tobacco Company, Richmond, Virginia.

Figure 43
A Light Smoke. Luckies - a light smoke of rich, ripe-bodied tobacco, 1937.
Electric bubble light in chrome case.
Charles H. Mullen, Stamford, Connecticut.

Figure 44
*Model **Lucky Strike Cigarette** Pavilion, American Tobacco Company, 1939 New York World's Fair*, 1939.
By J.J. Wenner, New York, New York.
Wood, plastic.
The American Tobacco Company, Richmond, Virginia.

Figure 45
Lucky Strike Green Has Gone to War! c. 1942.
Printed cardboard cigarette carton divider.
Warshaw Collection of Business Americana,
Archives Center,
National Museum of American History,
Smithsonian Institution, Washington, D.C.

Figure 46
Bell hop uniform, jacket, trousers, and cap, 1933-1974.
Belonging to Johnny Roventini.
The American Advertising Museum, Portland, Oregon.

Figure 47
Here's hoping for a Victorious Christmas next year. Call for Philip Morris, 1943.
Printed advertisement.
Private Collection.

Figure 48
Call for pleasure...call for Kent! , 1965.
Printed advertisement.
Better Homes and Gardens, March, 1965, back cover.
Valentine Museum.
Gift of Marvin Safir.
V88.148.9.

Figure 49
Winston Tastes Good - Like a Cigarette Should!, c. 1960.
Printed poster.
R.J. Reynolds Tobacco Company Archives, Winston-Salem, North Carolina.

Figure 50
The tobacco...the tip...and the taste! Hit Parade has all you want!, 1957.
Printed advertisement proof.
The American Tobacco Company, Richmond, Virginia.

Figure 51
No-To-Bac Kills the Tobacco Habit/Sold & Guaranteed by All Druggists,
c. 1900.
By Maxfield Parrish.
Lithograph on paper.
Philadelphia Museum of Art: The William H. Helfand Collection.
Philadelphia, Pennsylvania.

Figure 52
My Pleasure/My Choice, 1988.
Printed bumper sticker.
Valentine Museum.
Gift of Jane Webb Smith.
V88.181.6.
American Smokers Alliance/Guidelines for Smokers' Rights Groups,, 1989.
Printed pamphlet.
Valentine Museum.
V89.259.2.
American Smokers Alliance, 1989.
Printed matchbook.
Valentine Museum.
V89.259.3.
What Next/American Right to Smoke, 1988.
Printed card.
Valentine Museum.
Gift of Jane Webb Smith.
V88.181.5.
If you want to light up, speak up. , 1989.
Printed matchbook.
Valentine Museum.
V89.259.4.
The Great American Welcome, 1988-1989, 1989.
Printed sticker.
The Tobacco Institute, Washington, D.C.

Figure 53
Smoking and Health, Report of the Advisory Committee to the Surgeon General of the Public Health Service, 1964.
Washington, D.C.: U.S. Department of Health Education and Welfare.
Valentine Museum.
Gift of Benjamin Rapaport.
V88.155.27.

Figure 54
Marlboro, 1989.
Cardboard cutout figure.
Valentine Museum.
Gift of Philip Morris, U.S.A.
V89.244.4.

Figure 55
Marlboro, 1989.
Neon sign.
Valentine Museum.
Gift of Philip Morris, U.S.A.
V89.244.3.

Figure 56
Salem, the refreshest, 1988.
Proof of printed advertisement.
Valentine Museum.
Gift of R.J. Reynolds Tobacco Company.
V88.188.2.

Figure 57
Gives you a taste so pleasing to the palate. Pall Mall. Outstanding - and they are mild (translation) c. 1950.
Tin sign for Puerto Rican market.
The American Tobacco Company, Richmond, Virginia.

Figure 58
Salem Fresh. A Clear and Clean Feeling. America's No. 1 Menthol, Salem. (Translation), 1988.
Printed advertisement for Asian market.
R.J. Reynolds Tobacco Company, Winston-Salem, North Carolina.

IV. Transforming American Values

Figure 59
Poor Richard Improved , 1753.
By Richard Saunders (Benjamin Franklin). Philadelphia, Pennsylvania.
Department of Special Collections, Alderman Library, University of Virginia,
Charlottesville, Virginia.

Figure 60
*Credit card, **Thalhimers**, c. 1940.
With leather case.
Valentine Museum.
V89.242.

Figure 61
Every Wednesday, The New York Woman, 1936.
The New York Woman, October 7, 1936, Vol. 1, front cover.
Colleen Callahan, Richmond, Virginia.

BIBLIOGRAPHY

ADVERTISING: GENERAL/CIGARETTE

Cruse, A.J. *Cigarette Card Cavalcade.* London: Vausen and Wiles, Ltd., 1948.

Diamant, Lincoln. *Television Classic Commercials, The Golden Years, 1948-1958.* New York: Hastings House Publishers, 1971, 104-128.

Ellsworth, Scott. "Inventing *Marlboro:* A Historical Context." *Marlboro Oral History Project.* Washington, D.C.: National Museum of American History, 1986.

Ewen, Stuart. *Captains of Consciousness, Advertising and the Social Roots of the Consumer Culture.* New York: McGraw-Hill Book Company, 1976.

Fox, Stephen Russell. *The Mirror Makers: A History of American Advertising and Its Creators.* New York: William Monroe and Company, Inc., 1984.

Gray, Thomas A. and Barry K. Miller. *Golden leaves, R.J. Reynolds Tobacco Company and the Art of Advertising.* Winston-Salem, North Carolina: R.J. Reynolds Tobacco Company, 1986.

Jones, Edgar R. *Those Were the Good Old Days: A Happy Look at American Advertising, 1880-1930.* New York: Simon and Schuster, 1959.

Lears, T.J. Jackson. "Some Versions of Fantasy: Toward a Cultural History of American Advertising, 1880-1930." *Prospects* 9(1984): 349-405.

Lewine, Harris. *Good-Bye to All That.* New York: McGraw-Hill Book Company, Inc., 1970.

Marchand, Roland. *Advertising the American Dream, Making Way for Modernity, 1920-1940.* Berkeley, Los Angeles, and London: University of California Press, 1985.

Mullen, Chris. *Cigarette Pack Art.* London: Ventura Publishing, Ltd., 1979, 1984 edited by Gallery Press.

Pettit, Ernest L. *The Book of Collectible Tin Containers with Price Guide.* New York: Ernest Pettit, 1968.

Schild, Gary. *Tobacco Tin Tags.* Westbrook, Connecticut: Gary Schild, 1972.

Schudson, Michael. *Advertising, the Uneasy Persuasion, Its Impact on American Society.* New York: Basic Books, Inc., 1984.

Scott, Walter Dill. *The Theory of Advertising.* Boston: Small, Maynard and Company, 1908.

Streamlining America. Dearborn, Michigan: Henry Ford Museum and Greenfield Village, 1986.

Watkins, Julian Lewis. *The 100 Greatest Advertisements, Who Wrote Them and What They Did.* New York: Dover Publications, 1959.

MASS PRODUCTION AND CONSUMPTION HISTORY

Banner, Lois. *American Beauty.* New York: Alfred A. Knopf, 1983.

Boorstin, Daniel J. *The Americans: The Democratic Experience.* New York: Vintage Books, 1974.

Chandler, Alfred D. Jr. *The Visible Hand: The Managerial Revolution in American Business.* Cambridge and London: Belknap Press of Harvard University Press, 1977.

Douglas, Mary and Baron Isherwood. *The World of Good, Towards an Anthropology of Consumption.* New York and London: W.W. Norton and Company, 1979.

Fox, Richard Wightman and T.J. Jackson Lears, editors. *The Culture of Consumption: Critical Essays in American History, 1880-1980.* New York: Pantheon Books, 1983.

Horowitz, Daniel. *The Morality of Spending, Attitudes toward the Consumer Society in America, 1875-1940.* Baltimore and London: The Johns Hopkins University Press, 1985.

Hounshell, David. *From the American System to Mass Production, 1800-1932, The Development of Manufacturing Technology in the United States.* Baltimore: The Johns Hopkins University Press, 1988.

Kasson, John F. *Amusing the Million: Coney Island at the Turn of the Century.* American Century Series. New York: Hill and Wang, 1978.

Lears, T.J. Jackson. "From Salvation to Self-Realization, Advertising and the Therapeutic Roots of the Consumer Culture, 1880-1930," Richard Wightman Fox and T.J. Jackson Lears, editors. *The Culture of Consumption: Critical Essays in American History, 1880-1980.* New York: Pantheon Books, 1983.

__________. *No Place of Grace, Antimodernism and the Transformation of American Culture, 1880-1920.* New York: Pantheon Books, 1981.

McKendrick, Neil, John Brewer, and J.H. Plumb. *The Birth of a Consumer Society, the Commercialization of Eighteenth Century England.* Bloomington: Indiana University Press, 1982.

Meikle, Jeffrey L. *Twentieth Century Limited, Industrial Design in America, 1925-1939.* Philadelphia: Temple University Press, 1979.

Potter, David M. *People of Plenty, Economic Abundance and the American Character.* Chicago and London: The University of Chicago Press, 1954.

Riesman, David. *The Lonely Crowd, a Study of the Changing American Character.* New Haven and London: Yale University Press, 1950, ninth printing 1964.

Susman, Warren J. *Culture as History: The Transformation of American Society in the Twentieth Century.* New York: Pantheon Books, 1984.

Trachtenberg, Alan. *The Incorporation of America, The Culture and Society in the Gilded Age.* New York: Hill and Wang, 1982.

Wiebe, Robert H. *The Search for Order, 1877-1920.* American Century Series. New York: Hill and Wang, 1967.

Wilson, Richard Guy, Dianne H. Pilgrim, and Dickran Tashjian. *The Machine Age in America, 1918-1941.* New York: Brooklyn Museum with Harry N. Abrams, Inc., 1986.

RICHMOND/TOBACCO HISTORY

Beringer, Richard E., Herman Hattaway, Archer Jones, William N. Still, Jr. *Why the South Lost the Civil War.* Athens: University of Georgia Press, 1986.

Breen, T.H. *Tobacco Culture, The Mentality of the Great Tidewater Planters on the Eve of the Revolution.* Princeton: Princeton University Press, 1985.

Chesson, Michael B. *Richmond After the War, 1865-1890.* Richmond: Virginia State Library, 1981.

Dabney, Virginius. *Richmond, the Story of a City.* Garden City, New York: Doubleday and Company, Inc., 1976.

Downey, Fairfax. *Lorillard and Tobacco.* New York: P. Lorillard Company, 1951.

Flannagan, Roy C. *The Story of Lucky Strike.* New York: The American Tobacco Company, 1938.

Golden Jubilee: Fifty Years of Progressive Merchandising. Richmond, Virginia: Miller and Rhoads, 1935.

Heimann, Robert K. *Tobacco and Americans.* New York, Toronto, and London: McGraw-Hill Book Company, Inc., 1960.

Kolodny, Joseph. *4000 Years of Service, the Story of the Wholesale Tobacco Industry and Its Pioneers.* New York: Farrar, Straus and Young, 1953.

Kulikoff, Allan. *Tobacco and Slaves, The Development of Southern Cultures in the Chesapeake, 1680-1800.* Chapel Hill: University of North Carolina Press, 1986.

MacKercher, Daniel. *A Memorial Relating to the Tobacco Trade Offered to the Confederation of the Planters of Virginia and Maryland.* Williamsburg: William Parks, 1737.

Morrison, Andrew, editor. *The City on the James, Richmond, Virginia.* Richmond, Virginia: The Chamber of Commerce, 1893.

Robert, Joseph Clarke. *The Story of Tobacco in America.* Chapel Hill: University of North Carolina Press, 1949.

Robert, Joseph Clark. *The Tobacco Kingdom.* Durham, North Carolina: Duke University Press, 1938.

Silver, Christopher. *Twentieth Century Richmond, Planning, Politics, and Race.* Knoxville: University of Tennessee, 1984.

"Sold American!" The First Fifty Years. New York: The American Tobacco Company, 1954.

Tilly, Nannie Mae. *The Bright Tobacco Industry, 1860-1929.* Chapel Hill: University of North Carolina Press, 1948.

Tyler-McGraw, Marie and Gregg Kimball. *In Bondage and Freedom.* Richmond, Virginia: The Valentine Museum, 1988.

Virginia and Tobacco, a Chapter in America's Industrial Growth. Washington, D.C.: The Tobacco Institute, Inc., 1960.

PERIODICALS

Albright, Cheryl L., David G. Altman, Michael D. Slater, and Nathan Maccoby. "Cigarette Advertisements in Magazines: Evidence for a Different Focus on Women's and Youth Magazines." *Health Education Quarterly* 15 (Summer 1988): 225-233.

__________. "How an Unhealthy Product is Sold: Cigarette Advertising in Magazines, 1960-1985." *Journal of Communications* 37 (Autumn, 1987): 95-106.

Barmash, Isadore. "Strategies That Sell Everywhere." *The New York Times* 6 (October 24, 1989): D1.

Bonner, Lin. "Why Cigarette Makers Don't Advertise to Women." *Advertising and Selling* 7 (Oct. 20, 1926): 21-23.

Bridges, J. Malcomb. "The Golden Weed." *Richmond Magazine* (April, 1931): 7,17, 32-33.

Brown, Patricia Leigh. "Designers Worry about Self-Image." *The New York Times* 6 (Oct. 12, 1989), D23.

Brown, Robert H. "Cigarette Ads: Accent on Taste." *Printers' Ink* 289 (Dec. 18-25, 1964): 26-27.

Dabney, Virginius. "Lady Nicotine's 350th Birthday." *Virginia Cavalcade* 12 (Summer 1962): 22-32.

Fine, Gary Alan. "The Psychology of Cigarette Advertising." *Journal of Popular Culture* 8 (Winter, 1974): 153-165.

Gaines, William H., Jr. "Some Called It Treason." *Virginia Cavalcade* 1 (Summer, 1951): 39-43.

Gloede, William F. "Agency Execs Feel at Home in *Marlboro* Country." *Ad Age* (Aug. 1, 1985): 46-48.

Hemphill, Dr. W. Edwin. "Just Look at Richmond's Smoke!" *Virginia and the Virginia County* (January, 1952): 8-12, 42-47.

James, John Q. "When Richmond's Leaf Industry Was Saved by Men of Stout Heart." *Richmond Times Dispatch* (March 18, 1945): 1D.

Kilborn, Peter L. "Darman Issues Warning on 'Self-Indulgent' U.S." *The New York Times* 4 (July 21, 1989), 1.

Lohof, Bruce A. "The Higher Meaning of Marlboro Cigarettes." *Journal of Popular Culture* 3 (Winter, 1969): 443-450.

"Marlboro Makes a Direct Appeal." *Advertising and Selling* 8 (March 23, 1927): 25.

Miller, Lois Mattox and James Monahan. "The Facts Behind Filter-Tip Cigarettes." *The Reader's Digest* 71 (July, 1957): 33-39.

__________. "Wanted and Available — Filter Tips that Really Filter." *The Reader's Digest* 72 (Aug., 1957): 43-49.

Mobil Oil. "A Dose of Reality." *The New York Times* 6 (October 5, 1989), A31.

Riesman, David. "Some Questions about the Study of American Character in the Twentieth Century." *Annals of the American Academy of Political and Social Science* 370 (March, 1967): 36-47.

Rouse, Parke, Jr. "John Rolfe: The Faceless Hero." *The Commonwealth: the Magazine of Virginia* 29 (March, 1962): 17-20.

Shaw, Renata V. "Nineteenth Century Tobacco Label Art." *The Quarterly Journal of the Library of Congress* 28 (April, 1971): 76-102.

Starr, Michael. "Cigarette Smoking and Masculinity in America." *Journal of Popular Culture* 17 (Spring, 1984): 45-57.

Westbrook, Robert. "Consuming Images." *Reviews in American History* 16 (March, 1988) 85-92.